Working at a Rescue Mission

Just Another Day in Paradise

Donna Junker

GreenWine Family Books™
A division of GlobalEdAdvancePress

Books may be ordered at

www.gea-books.com/bookstore or

From the author at donnajunker@roadrunner.com

or any place good books are sold.

Published by
GreenWine Family Books
A division of

GlobalEdAdvance PRESS

This book is dedicated

To all my friends at the Lexington Rescue Mission:
Staff, volunteers, and clients,
Who taught me to truly appreciate God's love
In a much deeper and more profound way.

Thank you.

I invite you to enter with me into the daily life of working at a mission, discover why Gospel rescue missions are so important, and then meet some of the colorful people I came to know as you read these pages. To have physical needs met, the Christian Faith is never forced upon anyone.

The stories in this book are the unique experiences I had as Chaplain at the Lexington Rescue Mission (LRM); however, the programs that were implemented, the assistance that was given, and the ideas and philosophies that the LRM utilized can be helpful in any rescue mission, transitional house, or emergency homeless shelter.

Donna Junker

Table of Contents

"The world today is hungry not only for bread but hungry for love; hungry to be wanted, to be loved."

Inspirational Sayings of Mother Teresa card
Calcutta, India

Prologue

What is Love?

In 416 B.C., a banquet took place in the home of the
poet Agathon, with his friends Apollododros, Aristodemos,
Socrates, Agathon, Pausanias, Aristophanes, Eryximachos,
Phaidros, and Alcibiades. The conversation at this banquet is
found in the Platonic dialogue called the *Symposium*. Most of
us have at least heard of the philosopher Socrates, who asked
a great many questions at this banquet, where these thinkers
attempted to define love. In the ancient Greek culture in which
they lived, many gods were recognized, and the god of Love
was considered the "oldest, and most precious, and has the
most power to provide virtue and happiness for mankind, both
living and dead" (Rouse, 78). Love was considered to be a deity
whose father was Plenty and whose mother was Penury (*penury*
is defined as extreme poverty). Since Love is the son of Plenty
and Poverty, "he is always poor; and far from being tender
and beautiful, as most people think, he is hard and rough and
unshod and homeless, lying always on the ground without
bedding, sleeping by the doors and in the streets in the open air,
having his mother's nature, always dwelling with want.

But from his father again he designs upon beautiful and
good things, being brave and go-ahead and high-strung, a
mighty hunter, always weaving devices, and a successful coveter
of wisdom, a philosopher all his days, and great wizard and
sorcerer and sophist. He was born neither mortal nor immortal;
but on the same day, sometimes he is blooming and alive, when
he has plenty, sometimes he is dying; then again he gets new
life through his father's nature; but what he procures in plenty
always trickles away, so that Love is not in want nor in wealth,

and again is between wisdom and ignorance" (Rouse, 99). These philosophers continued to discuss their ideas of love at this banquet, as well as the origin of love. According to Socrates, Love is "A great spirit" (Rouse 98).

As a Christian, I consider the One True God, manifested in Jesus Christ to be love, since the Bible says, "*God is love*" (1 John 4:8 and 16). So, is love a deity as the ancient Greeks believed? Yes. The Bible says, "*God is love*" not only in 1 John, but basically throughout the Bible. Scripture continues to define love by saying, "*In this the love of God was made manifest among us, that God sent his only Son into the world, so that we might live through him. In this is love, not that we have loved God but that he loved us and sent his Son to be the propitiation for our sins. Beloved, if God so loved us, we also ought to love one another. No one has ever seen God; if we love one another, God abides in us and his love is perfected in us. By this we know that we abide in him and he in us, because he has given us of his Spirit*" (1 John 4:9-13). Is God a "great spirit" as Socrates said? Yes. John 4:24 says, "*God is spirit, and those who worship him must worship him in spirit and truth.*"

Plato wrote the Symposium, where he recorded the conversations of his friends (including Socrates) about love over four hundred years before the birth of Jesus, so of course there was no way they could have known about Christ. However, these ancient Greek thinkers thought of love as something divine.

In this book, we will define love through a Christian perspective, based on the Bible, but I will also focus on one aspect of love that came from the Symposium; that love is, poor and "far from being tender and beautiful as most people think." Love is also sometimes "hard and rough and unshod and homeless." It was in working at a rescue mission where I came to understand love in a different way, namely, the infinite love of God for very broken people.

Prior to working at the Mission, I never had extensive conversations with homeless people, nor the opportunity to really know people who live on the streets who often struggle with substance abuse, both drugs and alcohol, and some who never experienced or understood love, but all who greatly long for love. Sadly, since many homeless people feel unworthy of love, basically because they are often shunned by most people in society, they do not appreciate how much God loves them, no matter where their lives have taken them. It is difficult to grasp the love of God when one does not experience the love of a fellow human being.

Most of us may feel sadness or even pity for people who have no home, who might be hungry, dirty, and ill-clothed, and we think about the lack of their basic physical needs. However, in my almost six years of working as a chaplain at a mission, I have come to understand more fully something Mother Teresa once said, "The world today is hungry not only for bread but hungry for love; hungry to be wanted, to be loved" (Inspirational Sayings of Mother Teresa card at Calcutta, India). There is an empty hole in the hearts and lives of many of the people I met and came to know at the Mission that only the Great Spirit of Love could fill. As chaplain, my most difficult role was to get to know my clients, gain their trust, and then lead them to that infinite love of Jesus Christ, helping them to understand that there is a God who truly loves them, even in their messy lives. Saint Thomas Aquinas once said that to love is to will the good of another; that is a simple yet profound statement. When we meditate on what Aquinas said, it would change the way we live and treat other people, especially people who appear to be so different from us, such as the homeless. Love comes in very surprising and yet simple ways.

The late priest and author Henri Nouwen once taught at Harvard University. At the height of his distinguished career, he left Harvard and moved to a community called Daybreak near Toronto, Canada in order to take care of a young man named Adam. Many people think Adam's life was useless and that he should have been aborted. Nouwen described his friend like this:

"Adam is a 25-year-old man who cannot speak, cannot dress himself, cannot walk alone, cannot eat without much help. He does not cry or laugh. Only occasionally does he make eye contact. His back is distorted. His arm and leg movements are twisted. He suffers from severe epilepsy and, despite heavy medication, sees few days without grand-mal seizures. Sometimes, as he grows rigid, he utters a howling groan. On a few occasions I've seen a big tear roll down his cheek.

It takes me about an hour and a half to wake Adam up, give him his medication, carry him into his bath, wash him, shave him, clean his teeth, dress him, walk him to the kitchen, give him his breakfast, put him in his wheelchair and bring him to the place where he spends most of the day with therapeutic exercises" (Yancey, 120).

I have never had to care for someone like Adam, not even close, but there were people who came to the mission who had cerebral palsy, addictions, missing legs, blind, mental illnesses, and a variety of huge needs. We all have needs; some are just not as noticeable. Henri Nouwen said after leaving Harvard and working with Adam, "What makes us human is not our mind but our heart, not our ability to think but our ability to love" (Yancey, 120). Yes, I admit, some people are hard to love, but those are the people God places in our paths and commands us to love. The only way we can truly change lives is through loving people and trying to help people understand love when they have never experienced it for themselves; that in my opinion, is the primary role of a Christian rescue mission, and the primary role of all Christians everywhere. Nouwen wrote that it is "obligatory for Christians to offer an open and hospitable space where strangers can cast off their strangeness and become our fellow human beings" (Nouwen, Reaching Out, 43); rescue missions provide that space.

There were so many amazing people I met at the Mission, including the people who came in need for our services, (our clients) who sometimes tested my patience, sometimes drove me crazy, but who always taught me that we are all broken people, and despite our obvious, and not so obvious sins, God still loves us all completely. Perhaps it was in working at a rescue mission, getting to know the street people who came through our doors, and getting to love many of them, that God allowed me to become more human. As Nouwen said, it is not our intellect, but our hearts and our ability to love that truly makes us human. As in 1 Corinthians 13, without love, none of our work really matters. A Christian mission's main goal is to love all people who come through their doors and to share with them the love of our Savior, Jesus Christ. People see Jesus when they are loved, accepted, and heard, which is what we do.

The clients written about in this book have given me permission to tell their stories. Some of the names have been changed except where people wanted their real names used in the hopes that their powerful stories will glorify God and help you, the reader, perhaps better understand the need for faith-based missions. Some of their challenges in life and the battles they fought are also, of course, not unique to LRM but will be found in some form or fashion in other missions and shelters.

Welcome to a world with which many of you may not be very familiar and enjoy the journey.

O Jesus,
Grant that, even if you are hidden under the
unattractive disguise of anger, of crime, or of madness,
I may recognize you and say, "Jesus, you who suffer,
how sweet it is to serve you."

Give me, Lord, this vision of faith, and my work
will never be monotonous, I will find joy in harboring
the small whims and desires of all the poor who suffer...
What a privilege I am granted in being able to take care of you!

O God, since you are Jesus who suffers, deign to
be for me also a Jesus who is patient, indulgent with
my faults, who looks only at my intentions, which are
to love you and to serve you in the person of each
of these children of yours who suffer.
Lord, increase my faith.
Bless my efforts and my work,
now and forever."

(Portions of a prayer of Mother Teresa
No Greater Love, p. 183).

1

He's Not Dead

*"If you think you are too small to make a difference,
try sleeping in a closed room with a mosquito."*
An African Proverb

"It's o.k. He's not dead. I called 911." The lady at the
front desk spoke those words to me as I came to work one
morning when she saw me immediately stop to look at the man
crumpled up on the floor in the hallway outside the mission's
dining room. Relieved that the man was still breathing, and
help was on the way, I sat with him on the floor until the
paramedics arrived, and then thought, "What ever happened
to being greeted with 'good morning' when we come into
work, like most people?" You just never know what you will be
walking in to when you work at a rescue mission, and what will
unfold and occur throughout the workday. One thing is sure;
life at the mission is never boring.

My official title at the mission was Pastoral Care
Coordinator. I am an ordained chaplain and my ministry at
the mission was primarily that of a chaplain, which basically
entailed active listening, counseling, praying with the people
who came for help (we refer to them as our clients), developing
trusting relationships, and teaching. Of course, there were
always "other duties as assigned" of which were sometimes
quite unusual and messy. After graduating from seminary, I did
a one-year residency called Clinical Pastoral Education (CPE)
where chaplains are trained in hospitals to deal with various
crises as a "non-anxious presence," to be an active listener to
anyone who needs to be heard, and to learn the sometimes-
complicated ministry of chaplaincy. My previous CPE training

was invaluable at the mission since there were crisis's almost daily. I was also privileged to have training in de-escalation while working at the hospital, and considering the nature of a rescue mission, I relied on that information as well. I was sometimes referred to as the "mission bouncer" when clients became unruly, aggressive, or disrespectful and were asked to leave. At five foot five, 130 pounds, and a woman in her mid-50's, I was not an imposing physical threat to anyone, but calmly de-escalating a volatile situation demands firm words, respect, and yes, even love; after all, that is all our clients actually crave.

Over the years we saw many people come and go at the mission. There are the regular clients who come every day for years, and the mission is a regular part of their day; we often get to know these people fairly well. I worked in the building called the Outreach Center, where our doors are open to anyone from 9:00 a.m. until 5:00 p.m. Monday – Friday and 9:00 – 1:00 on Saturday. Sunday's the mission is closed. We also have two buildings for men's transitional housing, and one for women, staffed seven days a week, twenty-four hours a day. The men and women who live in these homes frequently come to the Outreach Center for the various services we provide. Coffee and donuts/snack bars are served from 9:00 – 10:00 each morning, and lunch is served from 12:00 – 1:00. All of the food served at the mission is free. Shelves are in the hallway outside of the lunchroom which often have bread, crackers, dry goods, fresh fruits and vegetables that anyone can take with them as well.

Three days a week we hold "walk-ins" where people can meet with a resource coordinator to have some basic needs met, such as: assistance with housing, make appointments for our jobs program, get a coat, hat, gloves or a rain poncho, receive hygiene products and emergency food, set up appointments with the local food pantry called "God's Pantry" for monthly groceries, get help obtaining identification (when people leave prison their identification is often missing), receive blankets, backpacks, tents, household supplies, socks, and shoes, bring their laundry, or just to talk with someone or pray. All of these items the mission has to give to our clients are donated or purchased from private cash donations. There are literally thousands of people who donate to the mission, including many individuals, churches, and businesses. There are also grant writers on staff who write grants for various different projects the mission is involved with, but very little government funding is utilized. The mission does accept some government grants, but only if they will not compromise the goals and heart of the mission. Sometimes the grant-writers have to walk away from large dollar government grants if they would require them to silence the Gospel. The mission seeks to share the Gospel of Jesus Christ with anyone who comes through their doors without any hinderances. God has always supplied for the needs of, not only the people who come for assistance, but also for staff salaries and the buildings the mission utilizes for their various services.

We have a hospitality room for our walk-in clients where they sign in and wait their turn for assistance, which always has water bottles, a pot of coffee and some snacks, in addition to Bibles and magazines. A volunteer sits in the hospitality room to visit with people as they desire and gives them a prepared piece of paper to fill out stating who they are and what they need. They are also given a prayer card to fill out with their prayer requests, if they have any.

When a person's name is called in the hospitality room, we take them to our prayer room which offers a private, quiet place to talk where I would often work. We also utilize several clergy members and mature Christian lay people who volunteer their time, usually once a week in the prayer rooms. We assure our clients that prayer is not necessary to have their physical needs met and would never force prayer or our faith upon people; rather we stress that we respect all people and offer to hear their stories and pray for them if they desire. The Gospel can never be forced. People see Jesus when they are loved, accepted, and heard, which is what we do, hoping to point them to the abundant life He wants for each one of us. Almost everyone though desired prayer, and some people would say, "Well I guess it can't hurt!" After a client leaves the prayer room, they see a resource coordinator who gives them (as much as possible), the physical things they request. The resource coordinators are usually social workers whose training allows them to navigate the sometimes complicated social and government systems.

There is a separate program called the Homeless Intervention Program (known as HIP) where a resource counselor helps individuals and families who are homeless move into their own home by providing financial assistance for the first month's rent, as well as individual budget counseling, resource referrals, and case management. As you can see, in addition to helping with emergency needs, the mission helps teach people to be self-sufficient and get back on their feet. Many of us have heard the African Proverb, "Give a man a fish, and he can eat for a day; teach a man to fish, and he can eat for a life-time;" that is what the mission hopes to achieve.

We also have chapel services five days a week, from 11:00 – 11:50. There were the "regulars" who would attend, but I would often go into the dining room each day to remind all of our clients about chapel and try to bring in others. In chapel, a Bible lesson is given and there is often lively conversation.

The mission employed another Pastoral Care Coordinator who worked twelve hours a week who would usually teach chapel. He was a pastor of over 40 years and was well respected and liked. When he was gone though, I would fill in and teach.

Every Wednesday we have a program called Steady Hands, which was modeled a bit after Celebrate Recovery. While I worked at the mission, Lee and his wife Beth were an integral part of Steady Hands and had volunteered in this capacity for many years. Lee later became a staff member, but continued to volunteer with Steady Hands, which was not a part of his regular work. Lee would normally open the evening with contemporary worship music (usually loud), with the words of each song up on a screen for everyone to follow or sing along if they wanted. Our clients seemed to enjoy the music along with prayer and praise time, together lasting about forty-five minutes. Lee reminded everyone to try to see God in their daily lives and to find something each day to praise Him for, which is a good habit we all should have!

After a ten-minute break, we gathered for a lesson and discussion based on Scripture that related to everyday matters and the struggles we all sometimes face; I would generally give this lesson. Sometimes I based the teaching on certain books which we used for our discussion, and sometimes we used various biblical video series, but the lessons were always based on the Christian life and Scripture. Occasionally we would have a movie night, where all we would do is play a Christian movie and serve popcorn and soft drinks. Whatever venue we chose, the evenings always end with a hot meal. Several different churches regularly volunteer to bring the meal, serve the food, and clean up when finished. What a blessing these churches are for us, and of course our clients really look forward to a great dinner each Wednesday. The meal is also a good time for fellowship and further discussion on the evening's lesson. Spiritual care, the presentation of the Gospel, and the love of Jesus Christ is an integral part of the work of the mission, of which I so appreciated.

Another large part of my work at the mission was pastoral counseling. Having been a former hospice chaplain, I had certification in grief counseling, which I often utilized. Many of our clients experienced great losses during their lives: loved ones who died (often from an overdose or through violence), losses of children who were taken away by the state since they were unable to care for them, losses of homes, families, jobs, and often, losses of self... the most difficult loss, and one that is so important to regain. What do I mean by a loss of self? After enough sadness, loss, disappointments, lack of direction, loneliness, and a basic lack of love, many of our clients said they turned to drugs and/or alcohol abuse to ease their pain. Consequently, they never discover their God-given talents and purpose in life, and simply drift through each day as they watch the years go by, getting old and never realizing who they actually are and what God placed them on this earth to do. "Know thyself" is a philosophical maxim that so many people never actualize, and they lose themselves in the messiness of life. I wrote a recovery program and book entitled, *"Recovery: a Return to the Self"* that deals with this issue of self-loss. God created all of us to fulfill a role on this earth, and I wonder how many of us ever fulfill that role, especially the people who come to a rescue mission.

Part of the work of a rescue mission is to care for basic physical needs, like food, clothing, and shelter. However, once those needs are met, the spiritual care takes place to assist clients in discovering who they are and why they exist, and then more importantly, who God is and what He is like. You cannot lead a starving person to Christ, but once basic needs are met, you can begin to expand their ideas of what life is all about. Of course, basic psychology recognizes human needs and drives which a mission can incorporate into their work, and then bring people along to higher levels in their lives, such as thinking about their spiritual natures and the meaning and purpose of their lives, rather than just basic survival.

The psychologist Abraham Maslow wrote a paper in 1943 entitled "A theory of Human Motivation" in the journal *Psychological Review*, about self-actualization and what he called a hierarchy of needs. Maslow created a classification system which reflected the universal needs of society as its base and then proceeding to more acquired emotions. There are five levels of Maslow's Hierarchy of Needs, which are:

1. *Physiological or Basic Needs*. Physiological needs are universal human needs. Efforts to accomplish higher needs may be interrupted temporarily by a deficit of basic, primal needs, such as a lack of food or air. Physiological needs are considered an internal motivation according to Maslow's hierarchy of needs. Maslow's idea is that humans are compelled to fulfill these physiological needs first if they are ever going to pursue intrinsic satisfaction on a higher level. To pursue needs higher up Maslow's hierarchy, physiological needs must be met first. This means that if a human is struggling to meet their physiological needs, then they are unlikely to pursue safety, belongingness, esteem, and self-actualization. Physiological needs include air, water, food, sex, sleep, health, clothing, and shelter.

Obviously, many of the people who come to a rescue mission lack these basic needs such as food, water, clothing and shelter, which are the first and most basic needs we can provide. Many very kind and generous people donate material items to the mission such as food, clothing, hygiene supplies, water, etc. which are all needed and appreciated. A cold, dirty, hungry person does not care about much more than getting warm, fed, and clean. These basic human needs are where a rescue mission begins, but of course must then move on to other human needs.

2. *Safety and Security Needs.* Once a person's physiological needs are relatively satisfied, their safety needs take precedence and dominate their behavior. People want safety and stability. The absence of physical safety might arise from family violence or childhood abuse, and the absence of economic stability might be due to an economic crisis or lack of work opportunities or training. In our case at the mission, many people cannot hold a job due to substance abuse issues. This second level is more likely to occur in children as they generally have a greater need to feel safe. This second level includes: shelter, job security, health, and safe environments. If a person does not feel safe in an environment, they will seek safety before attempting to meet any higher level of survival. Safety needs include personal safety, emotional security, financial security, and well-being.

In the case of our clients (some who are homeless, and others who are housed but who live in dangerous neighborhoods), they do not have these safety needs met. In the mission's attempt to find work for people and get them housed, this need for safety and security can be met. Also, just keeping the building open during the day for people to be in and offering a listening ear is a way of providing for this need as well.

3. *Love and Belongingness.* This is the satisfaction that comes from knowing you are not alone and that you have somebody to relate to. After physiological needs (level 1) and safety needs (level 2) are met, the third level of human needs is

interpersonal and involves feelings of belongingness. According to Maslow, humans possess a need for a sense of belonging and acceptance among social groups, regardless of whether these groups are large or small. For example, some large social groups may include clubs, co-workers, religious groups, professional organizations, sports teams, gangs, and online communities. Some examples of small social connections include family members, intimate partners, mentors, colleagues, and confidants. According to Maslow, humans need to love and be loved – both sexually and non-sexually by others. Many people become susceptible to loneliness, social anxiety, and clinical depression in the absence of this love or belonging element (which is a large part of being homeless). This need is especially strong in childhood, and it can override the need for safety as witnessed in children who cling to abusive parents. Deficiencies due to hospitalization, neglect, shunning, ostracism, etc. can adversely affect an individual's ability to form and maintain emotionally significant relationships in general. Social belonging needs include family, friendship, and intimacy. This need for belonging may overcome the physiological and security needs, depending on the strength of the peer pressure. In contrast, for some individuals, the need for self-esteem is more important than the need for belonging, while for others, the need for creative fulfillment may supersede even the most basic needs.

At the mission, we see so many people go from one relationship to the next, often very quickly, in an attempt to feel loved, a strong and basic human need indeed. Some women who are viewed as promiscuous are simply trying to fulfill this basic human need and do not really know how. These women have no basic understanding of what real love is and have probably never experienced love. Philip Yancey wrote in his book, *The Jesus I Never Knew* that the great author Dostoevsky said he "came to believe that only through being loved is a human capable of love" (Yancey, 141). Even the Bible says, "*We love because he* (God) *first loved us*" (1 John 4:19). Perhaps the reason we see some people who seem almost incapable of love is because they have never experienced love themselves. People who grow up in very dysfunctional homes, homes where drug use is present, or homes where the parent(s) have never experienced love (and are therefore incapable of giving or showing love), is the reason some people are homeless and incapable of forming real relationships. The hunger for love is present in everyone, but the ability to truly love often must be learned.

4. *Esteem Needs.* Most people have a need for a stable self-esteem, which is based on real capacity or achievement. Maslow noted two versions of esteem needs. The "lower" version of esteem is the need for respect from others, and may include a need for status, recognition, fame, prestige, and attention. The "higher" version of esteem is the need for self-respect, and can include a need for strength, competence, mastery, self-confidence, independence, and freedom.

I have never met a homeless person who had a good sense of esteem or self-respect, but instead, most of our clients feel like failures and "rejects" in society. When this need is not met, many people, especially young men, turn to gangs where they feel a sense of esteem from fellow gang members. Also, perhaps those clients who choose to remain homeless are in a distorted way trying to meet their needs of independence and freedom, which some of our clients have said does indeed come from living on the streets; surely, we can point them to another way. I often attempted to show clients their inherent worth (which hopefully leads to self-esteem) as being made in the image of God and loved by Him, and also the freedom that can be found in Christ, rather than from a secular/psychological point of view. 2 Corinthians 3:17 says *"Where the Spirit of the Lord is, there is freedom,"* and Jesus said in John 8:32 that *"The truth will set you free."*

5. *Self – Actualization.* Maslow wrote, "What a man can be, he must be" (Maslow, 91). This quotation forms the basis of the perceived need for self-actualization and refers to the need to realize one's full potential. Maslow described this as the desire to accomplish everything that one can, and to become the most that one can be (Maslow, 92). People may have a strong desire to become an ideal parent, to succeed athletically, or to create paintings, pictures, or inventions (Maslow, 93). In order to understand this level of need, a person must not only succeed in the previous needs but also master them. People who are motivated to pursue this last goal want to understand how their needs, their relationships, and their sense of self are expressed through their behavior. Self-actualization needs include partner acquisition, parenting, utilizing and developing talents and abilities, pursuing goals, and transcendence. Maslow defines "transcendence," as altruism or spirituality, and a desire to reach the infinite above.

At the mission, there is a great emphasis on a person's spiritual nature and in finding and knowing God, which for a Christian, is Jesus Christ. According to Maslow, these five needs listed above are met in the order listed, and a person cannot achieve number five for example, if the preceding four are not met. Maslow believed many people never reach level five. Even the secular world understands that all people have a need for meaning and purpose in life, and only after their basic physical and psychological needs are met can a person pursue deeper needs such as the purpose of their lives, the existence and/or nature of God, and other spiritual matters, of which we all have.

At the mission, we try to meet all of those needs, including most importantly, the spiritual hunger and needs that people do indeed possess. One way I attempted to meet these higher needs was through talking with people, getting to know them, making them feel cared for and loved, and in counseling sessions where we could explore some of their issues on a deeper level.

During my employment at the mission, I worked towards certification in Christian drug and alcohol counseling, which of course was very much needed in my role. Alcohol abuse and illicit drug use are often the result of the emptiness in people's lives, their unmet needs of all kinds and the pain that accompanies many of them; not knowing how to cope with pain, many of our clients simply mask those negative feelings with drugs. Some clients also spoke of physical pains for which they self-medicated since many did not seek proper medical care.

Counseling sessions were frequently scheduled based on simple conversations I had with our clients who opened up to me and needed someone to hear their stories and try to make sense of their lives. Counseling referrals also came from the prayer room where many people poured out their hearts and souls, confessed their sins, and allowed themselves to be vulnerable in the private and sacred space of that prayer room. Sometimes a client simply wrote "help" on their prayer card, which led to further counseling. Sometimes something as simple as, "Pray for me to have a better life," was written on the prayer card, and counseling sessions explored ways in which a person could improve their life. Many prayer cards had something sad written on them such as, "Please pray my kids will get something for Christmas." One woman named Christy, wrote, "Without a home, no family, no support, sometimes I doubt and get discouraged to not stay sober. I'm doing it though, but still haven't come to terms with my husband's death last year, though I know I need to accept it. Being homeless and without friends and without anyone's support has also been very difficult to accept." This prayer card shows how Maslow's hierarchy of needs were not met for Christy, as she expressed her lack of basic physiological needs, her desire for psychological needs to be met such as safety and security, and of course her need and desire for love and belonging.

Since so many of the people who come to a rescue mission abuse drugs, the staff were all trained in administering Narcan which is used when a person overdoses from an opiate. We all kept Narcan in our desk drawers to use as needed. There were several times where we did indeed administer Narcan while we waited for the EMS to show up and take over to (hopefully) save the lives of our clients, like the man lying in the hallway. He survived.

Many of our clients who abuse drugs were brought up in homes where drug use was rampant, and this was "normal" life to them. One of our clients, Kathy, told me she was trying to rebuild her life. She said she was living with her mother who was actively using drugs, which of course hindered her own recovery. Kathy needed to get away from her mom, but she did not have the money for her own apartment. I asked Kathy if she wanted a job, but she was unsure if she could even hold a job and knew she was ill-prepared. Kathy's mom never worked but spent her days using drugs and getting high. Kathy never knew her dad. Living a sober life and getting up to go to a job every day was a very foreign concept, not only for Kathy, but for a lot of our clients.

The mission has a job placement service called *Advance Lexington* where staff train clients for the work force and help find jobs for anyone who wants to work. They partner with local businesses who hire workers on a temporary or permanent basis through their staffing service. The staff conduct initial employment assessments to help clients identify potential employers, and program participants receive help with their job search, including assistance with creating resumes and cover letters, fill out online job applications, procure proper clothing for interviews, and receive bus passes as needed to get to their interviews. Unfortunately, many of our clients have never worked, failed drug tests when they did apply for work, and never held any kind of responsibility or disciplined themselves to be at a certain place, at a specific time each day. Many of us take for granted that we work, we rent an apartment or buy a house because we were raised in a "normal" environment where this was modeled for us. It is surprising how many people have never woken up to an alarm clock with somewhere to go each day. Basically, we are usually products of our environment and upbringing, and what is a "normal" life greatly varies from person to person.

There are a lot of people who desire a better life, but they have no idea how to obtain it and what steps are needed, especially when their lives consist of basic survival, where Maslow's level one needs are not even met. As the mission attempts to meet these basic physiological needs, we hope to move onto the next levels. As a chaplain who focused primarily on levels three, four and five, the goal was to work with colleagues to meet levels one and two, although our work often overlapped in our respective roles.

There were some clients, perhaps the exceptions and not the rule, who preferred to be homeless. I know that is difficult for many people to believe, but it is in fact true. While one of the goals of any rescue mission is to get people back on their feet so to speak, to help them become sober, to assist them in finding work, dignity, and self-respect, and of course most importantly, to find Jesus, not all people actually want that for themselves. As a chaplain, I wanted to know why, and how that might change, so I spent much of my time simply talking to clients and getting to know them.

John was a regular client who had come to the mission for years, mostly for lunch and for a place to stay during the day to get out of the heat, the rain, or the cold. He lived under a bridge or in a tent in a wooded area for eleven years and did not want a home. The only ambition he had was to collect aluminum cans every day, take them to the recycling center, and get paid enough cash to get a few snacks at the gas station and to buy drugs. John was a very kind man, and I really liked him. He was in his early 30's and I told him we could get him a job, as well as an apartment, but he was not interested. He thanked me and said, "I'm happy collecting my cans and living in my tent. I've lived this way for so long now, it's all I know." When I asked John about living outside when it rained or in the winter when it gets cold, he told me "You get used to it." When I inquired about what he might do when he was old, John said he did not think about the future. Poverty is a day-to-day existence, and that is about as far as plans go. When getting high dominates a person's life, there is not much else to aspire towards.

Damon was a regular client who preferred to live in a wooded area in his tent. He rode his bike to the mission for lunch every day and was strong and in good physical shape. Damon was in his early 40's and fully capable of working but he said he did not want a job when I asked to get him into our jobs program. I gained Damon's trust and we had meaningful conversations almost every day, as he was an intelligent and interesting man. Damon also had a sordid background of drug abuse in his family and broken and volatile family relationships.

His father was physically abusive to him most of his life and he never felt love from either his mother or father.

Despite being homeless, Damon liked to stay neat and clean. Once a week he would bring his dirty clothes to the mission since we had a laundry service for the homeless, and he would keep his clean clothes in a clean garbage bag that we supplied, and his dirty clothes in another bag. Of course, I asked Damon about housing, but he preferred to stay alone in his tent. One day Damon came to me very upset because he woke up that morning and found three other tents in his area; he lost his solitude. Damon was also afraid that with the other tents in his secluded camp, the police would find them and make them move; this was Damon's home and he wanted to protect it. One morning on my way to work as I drove past Damon's camp, all the bushes and trees were cut down and his tent was gone, along with the other tents. Damon did not show up at the mission that day and I was worried about him. I asked around and found out that the city cleared the land because of all the tents that were set up in this area as a homeless camp, and Damon was arrested for an outstanding warrant. Some people do not want jobs or housing because they do not want to be found and arrested for their outstanding warrants. Being homeless is a way to remain anonymous.

Almost two years after Damon disappeared from his camp, I walked into the mission and Norris, our maintenance worker grabbed me by the arm and said, "Oh Donna, someone is really anxious to see you. Come here!" I followed Norris out the side door wondering who wanted to see me, and to my surprise, there was Damon! He turned and smiled at me, got up and gave me a big hug. I could not believe it! I told Damon that I had been thinking about him from time to time and wondered where he was, and how happy I was to finally see him. He told me that a couple of winter's ago he felt really cold living in his tent, and on a February day, he found a policeman sitting in his car and asked the officer to take him to jail. When the officer asked why, he said he was cold and tired of trying to hide. He said he had a warrant on him from a past charge and was ready to serve his time and get it passed him. The officer looked him up, found his information to be true, and took him to jail. Damon said he spent about 14 months in jail and then went to a halfway house in another town. When he completed that program, the case worker who was assigned to him wanted to find him an apartment in this other town, but Damon refused. He said he wanted to get back to the rescue mission to see me and another worker who he said, "really cared about people" and he wanted to be around us. What Damon did not know, was that I had recently retired from the mission as their chaplain, but that I simply could not stay away because I loved the people and came back on a volunteer basis; today was my volunteer day! Damon said, "See what I mean? You do really care." When God places love in our hearts for others, especially unbelievers, it is noticed. We all long for love, and that is the greatest thing that can actually change a person.

Damon had several health issues that he was trying to get taken care of and was working with a social worker who was trying to find him an apartment near the mission. I told him that we could get him in touch with the mission's employment services and get him a job, of which he finally agreed. I then said, after all of that is taken care of, then we'll focus on your soul. "I'd love to baptize you someday" I told him. He laughed and said, "Nature is all I need. Besides, I treat people kindly. I'm a nice guy. That's all I need to get to Heaven, right?" "No" I said. Just then a man walked by and said, "You need Jesus brother!" Damon said he did not understand all of that "religious stuff." I was on my way out, taking another client someplace, but I told Damon that we would talk when I returned and I would explain the Gospel to him in simple terms that did not sound complicated. He laughed. Damon knew I cared about him despite his apathy to my faith. He also knew the mission would help him and welcome him, no matter what he believed or did not believe. Like Jesus, we must "honor the dignity of people, whether he agreed with them or not" (Yancey, 244). Mostly, Damon knew he was loved as a human being by Christian people at a mission. I do not know if Damon will remain homeless; he said he prefers to live outside in nature, but the cold winters are difficult. I pray he gets on his feet, gets a job, moves into an apartment, and of course, finds the Lord. Unfortunately, he disappeared again. We plant the seeds and pray.

She went by the name of "Sidewalk" and would never reveal her name to me. Sidewalk was an avid hitchhiker and had numerous tattoos on her face. When I asked her about them, she said they represent each state she has hitch-hiked to, which were many. Sidewalk did not call herself homeless, but said she was "house-free" and wished to remain that way. I wondered what she was running from and was curious about her story, but she would not share anything more of her life. Sidewalk was young, probably in her 30's, but she had no teeth, had worn, wrinkled skin, and only one ambition in life – to hitch-hike to Hawaii. Since Hawaii is of course an island, I asked how that was possible, and she said, "You can hitch-hike onto a trash barge, you know the barges that dump trash in the ocean? Yah, they really do that! Lots of people get to Hawaii that way, and that is what I want to do!" I never saw Sidewalk again and wonder if she made it to Hawaii amongst a bunch of trash– her only dream in life. Drugs definitely take away dreams and aspirations to do something with one's life.

Frank was a very interesting client who was semi-regular for years. He was in his mid-sixties and had been homeless for years. He was kind, funny, and liked to talk with me. I learned that he had several grown children and grandchildren, all of whom he loved and kept in contact with and stayed with from time to time, but he preferred to be homeless. Frank said he did not like to be confined to living within four walls and did not want the responsibilities of having to pay rent and utility bills; he found freedom away from all responsibility. He occasionally used drugs, though not as much as he did when he was young, but he drank a lot of alcohol which was now his biggest vice. I would often see Frank stumbling around outside, going through dumpsters and trash cans looking for food – or whatever. He was normally sober when he came to the mission and we had very interesting and lively conversations about his life, his family, his past, and about what he wanted for his future. The concept of a future though, is often not considered amongst many of our clients, as life is simply a day-to-day existence. The future consisted of where their next meal might be found that day, and where they can find some drugs, and that is about as far as it went. Life was lived in the present, and that was hard enough.

Perhaps for some people it's easy to go through life without hopes and dreams, or to have very small ones that are easier to obtain. Dan had a girlfriend once who he really loved and had hopes of marrying and having a somewhat "normal" life. When she left him and broke his heart, he decided he would never be hurt again, and retreated to a life of solitude in his tent. Self-preservation is strong amongst many homeless people who protect themselves in their own little bubble, away from society, away from commitments, away from obligations, away from failures. Alcohol abuse and drugs allow an escape from the pain that many people do not know how to deal with, and some people no longer even have the desire and strength to seek help.

Some of the clients I spoke to did not see being homeless as a failure, but simply as a means to prevent failure. Why is it that some of us can fail, perhaps at many things, yet get back up and keep trying until we succeed, while others experience maybe only one failure, then quit so as not to fail again? How many homeless people were told by their parent(s) that they would never amount to anything, and were never given any examples of "success" or more so, any love and feelings of confidence and self-worth? I like to say, "Dream big, for we serve a big God" who wants us to lead lives that are meaningful and rich. Jesus said He came to bring us life, and life in abundance (John 10:10). If we do not believe in Jesus or trust in Him, or if God is very small for us and not the actual infinite and enormous God whose vastness we cannot even begin to wrap our heads around, then maybe our dreams also shrink to nothing more than collecting cans and riding trash barges.

The main issue with most of the people who come through the doors of a mission is that they have no dreams, no hopes, no aspirations to do anything with their lives, and have substance abuse problems. The stories I have told, and will continue to tell throughout this book, often revolve around drugs or alcohol abuse. One of the main goals of the staff was to try to get people sober so they could see past their day to day survival; unfortunately, that was incredibly difficult. Working at a rescue mission is not easy work, and there are constant spiritual battles.

Rescue missions exist for the glory of God, to share His love with each person who comes through the doors, to show the love of Jesus and help people see that we are all created in God's image and have a purpose for our lives, no matter how much of a mess someone's life might be currently. The mission is there to assist people at all levels: basic physical needs such as food, clothing, and shelter, and then onto the deeper needs of learning to work, live independently, and to know the love of Jesus Christ. Rescue missions cannot change and save everyone, but for those who do change, and especially for those who give their lives to Christ, they are eternally grateful for the mission.

I appreciate the wisdom of Mother Teresa who once said, *"We can do no great things; only small things with great love"* (inspirational sayings of Mother Teresa brochure given to me in Calcutta, India at the Missionaries of Charity). Perhaps many of our clients, and perhaps even those of you reading this book think that in order to be useful in this world we need to accomplish great things and impact many people; most of us do not. We have a sphere of influence that might only be as large as our homes, our neighborhoods, our churches, and maybe our workplaces. We can focus on doing the small things in life, but as Mother Teresa said, with great love. That is the work of a rescue mission. We see so many people come and go, in addition to our "regulars." We feed our clients a meal, we give them a pair of shoes, a coat, or some hygiene products, we give them a clean bathroom to use, or we wash their clothes. We smile and we hug. We listen and we pray. We do small things, with great love, and that is what changes people.

**Unfortunately, when there are too many
broken dreams, many people simply
give up dreaming.**

2

Afraid to Fail

"It is not the critic who counts, not the man who points out where the strong stumbled, or how the doer could have done better. The credit belongs to the man in the arena, his face marred by dust, who strives valiantly, who errors and falls short again and again: there is no effort without error. But he who tries, who knows the great enthusiasms, the great devotions, who spends himself in a worthy cause, at best knows the triumph of achievement, and at worst, failure while daring. His place shall never be with those cold and timid souls who know neither victory nor defeat."

Teddy Roosevelt

Brennan Manning wrote a book in 2005 entitled *The Ragamuffin Gospel*, along with Charles Brock who is a graphic designer and art director. Manning was a Korean War veteran and former Franciscan priest who held various academic and ministry positions in several universities and colleges. He traveled widely to preach and teach primarily about the unconditional love we have in Jesus Christ. Brennan Manning invited the late, great singer/song writer Rich Mullins to a quiet retreat with him to dig deeper into the love of Jesus. Both men were Christians who deeply loved the Lord, yet both struggled with alcoholism. In his *Ragamuffin Gospel* book, Manning wrote, "Often I have been asked, 'Brennan, how is it possible that you became an alcoholic after you got saved?' It is possible because I got battered and bruised by loneliness and failure; because I got discouraged, uncertain, guilt-ridden, and took my eyes off Jesus" (no page numbers in book). The last part of Manning's quote reminds me of the disciple Peter, who asked

Jesus if he could walk on water with Him, but when he took his eyes off Jesus, and saw the reality of what he was doing – walking on water – he began to sink (Matthew 14:28-31). Manning admitted that when he took his eyes off Jesus, he too sank, mostly into despair and alcoholism.

Some of our clients truly love Jesus, like Brennan Manning and Rich Mullins, but allow the bruising and battering of their lives to take their eyes off Jesus too, and often get caught up in addictions. Manning goes on to write in his book that after reading the gospel of Luke he thought, "Jesus spent a disproportionate amount of time with people described in the Gospels as the poor, the blind, the lame, the lepers, the hungry, sinners, prostitutes, tax collectors, the persecuted, the downtrodden, the captives, those possessed by unclean spirits, all who labor and are heavy burdened, the rabble who know nothing of the law, the crowds, the little ones, the least, the last, and the lost sheep of the house of Israel. In short, Jesus hung out with ragamuffins." (No page number given). In my opinion, Manning described most of our clients in that last quote, and that is why I loved my work at the rescue mission; people so in need of love, but not feeling worthy of love, especially from God. It was my desire to show them how much they were truly loved, and that they could indeed find freedom, forgiveness, hope, and change – even though they were "ragamuffins."

There is a hunger in all people for love, for acceptance, and for purpose. There is a hole in all people that only God can fill; some people understand that but feel unworthy of God's love and run away from God. Many people struggle with self-esteem and live with a poor self-image, which often leads to failure. When a person does not love themself or see any redeeming quality in themself, it is almost impossible to think God can love them. With such low self-esteem, anyone's life can become messy. One man, Joe, wrote on his prayer card that he handed me as he came into the prayer room, "My life is a mess. I need the Lord." That was all he wrote, so we talked about why his life was a mess and how he could change it, or rather, how the Lord could change it. Joe, like so many others I spoke with, had poor self-esteem and was afraid of failure, since, in his mind, he had failed so many times in the past and just could not "get it right." With little to no sense of self-worth, Joe felt like anything he attempted would fail. After a while, people like Joe stop trying.

One of the most common "failures" I heard about at the mission was when people with addictions went to rehab and then relapsed, which was very common. Another "failure" was being fired from a job. There were also relational "failures" of divorce or an inability to hold a relationship for very long. Some people lost houses and children and felt like they failed as parents. There were many perceived failures in our clients lives that sometimes paralyzed them from trying any more. All of the mission staff encouraged our clients to keep trying, no matter how many times they failed.

I often told my clients that many very famous people failed numerous times, yet they went on to do great things. Abraham Lincoln often failed when he ran for various public offices. Lincoln lost many elections, but he kept trying until he became president, and one of our greatest! I read about the famous author Leo Tolstoy who appeared to be very afraid of failure. He aimed at perfectionism but lived his life with an almost constant fear of failure and never found any peace. "Tolstoy's ardent strides toward perfectionism never resulted in any semblance of peace or serenity. Up to the moment of his death his diaries and letters kept circling back to the rueful theme of failure" (Yancey, 138).

I wanted to see my clients have peace in their lives, and this fear of failure in so many of them kept them from having that peace. I often told them that no matter how hard we try, we cannot attain perfection and we will all fail sometimes, including me. The secret is getting up and trying again after our failures. Mother Teresa once said, "Do not allow yourselves to be disheartened by any failure as long as you have done your best" (No Greater Love, 30). The secret though for many of our clients is trying to get them to actually do their best, and to encourage them along the way. We can get past our failures and live productive lives as we learn from our failures, rather than have those failures incapacitate us and keep us from even trying. I have a quote hanging in my house from the British author, professor, and theologian C.S Lewis that says, "For broken dreams, the cure is, Dream again." There are indeed many broken dreams amongst our clients at the mission, which they viewed as failures. I, along with all of the staff, encouraged people to dream again.

Author and Christian psychologist Gary Collins believes that failure sometimes comes not because someone tried and failed, but because others expect the person to fail. One example could be that parent who tells their child they will never amount to anything, or that teacher who conveys to their student that they are not very bright. For some people, these negative attitudes towards them makes them try even harder to prove their critic wrong and they go on to achieve many accomplishments in their lives. For other people though, such as many of the people who come to the mission, they conclude that since they are not expected to succeed, there is really no purpose in even trying. "With this attitude, nothing is ventured, so nothing is gained. Failure is assured, and self-esteem erodes even further" (Collins, 431). Unfortunately, this was the case in several of my clients of whom we tried to help.

Professional counselor Robert McGee wrote in his book, *The Search for Significance,* "Perhaps we find some strange kind of comfort in our personal failings. Perhaps there is some security in accepting ourselves as much less than we can become. That minimizes the risk of failure. Certainly, if we expect little from ourselves, we will seldom be disappointed!" (McGee, 96).

Fear of failure is closely tied to self-esteem. The Bible teaches that all human beings have intrinsic worth because we are created in God's image. "Since we are created in God's image, we possess great value and significance – not because of what we think about ourselves or what we have made of ourselves but because of how we were made by God" (Collins, 427). Trying to get a homeless person to see themselves in a positive light is not very easy. Using Scripture, I would attempt to show my clients that they have worth because God believes they have worth; after all, Jesus died for them and longs to live with them in eternity. We can find self-worth when we discover that we are loved by God, and that He desires us to love Him in return. When a person does not feel love and acceptance from other people though, it is very difficult to feel love and acceptance from God.

Fear of failure is also tied to feelings of shame. Some people believe they are inherently bad and can never change, so they do not even try. Women who have been sexually abused often feel shame, as if maybe the abuse was their fault. Women who are prostitutes, usually stemming from a drug habit, also feel shame. When a person thinks they are trapped in some shameful life-style, such as prostitution, their sense of who they can be often fades away and they look upon themselves as something dirty and worthless.

For several months in our Steady Hands teaching, I taught from a book called, *Who I am in Christ* by Neil Anderson. In using this book, we tried to get our clients to believe that they could be someone other than just their sin, but instead they could become a new creation in Christ. The goal was to turn their shame into repentance and renewal and to discover who they could be in Christ. 2 Corinthians 5:17 says, *"If anyone is in Christ, he is a new creation. The old has passed away; behold, the new has come."* Finding new life in Christ is what breaks people free from their fears, their consistent failures, and their low self-esteem. Neil Anderson wrote, "The most important belief that we possess is a true knowledge of who God is. The second most important belief is who we are as children of God, because we cannot consistently behave in a way that is inconsistent with how we perceive ourselves. And if we do not see ourselves as God sees us, then to that degree we suffer from a wrong identity and a poor image of who we really are" (Anderson, 11). Knowing who we are, or who *we can* be in Christ, is where we find our self-worth. We all worked hard at the mission to help people feel a sense of self-worth, love, and acceptance as we spent time with them. As the chaplain, I wanted our clients to realize that I truly wanted to know them as individuals, that I cared about them, and I stressed God's love for them as being made in His image.

There is a man named Scott who works for the city as an overdose prevention coordinator who I greatly respect and became friends with over the years. He regularly came to the mission from time to time to tell people about drug and alcohol rehabilitation programs and tried to get them into these various programs. He was always available when I called him after speaking to a client who was interested in rehab. As soon as his busy schedule allowed, Scott would come to the mission, talk to a client, and get him or her into a program. Everyone liked Scott since he is kind and easy to talk to and he understood the struggles so many of our clients faced. Unfortunately, many clients know they need rehab and want to get sober but are reluctant because they are afraid to fail at just one more thing, especially if they had been in rehab before and relapsed. Nothing ventured, nothing gained. However, I tried to stress something the Bible consistently teaches and a quote I had once read that said, "Nothing forces us to remain in the mold of the past. By the grace and power of God, we can change!" (McGee, 96).

Darryl was a client who came to the mission for months but would never open up and talk with me. He always appeared angry and frustrated, though I did not know why since he would not speak to me. Each day I saw Darryl, I would say hello, sometimes tap him on the shoulder and joke around with him, hoping he would someday speak to me; finally, after several months, he did. I invited him to our Wednesday evening program, Steady Hands, and told him he would get a nice dinner there. Darryl was hungry, so he stayed at the mission that afternoon and waited for the program to begin. He said he enjoyed Steady Hands and he became a regular for a while. Darryl never spoke at length to me or opened up about his life, but he did say he was homeless and in need of rehab. I called Scott, and on that November day, off he went to rehab to begin a new chapter in his life. I had not heard from Darryl for many months, but Scott said he was doing well and working full time. I appreciated how Scott checked on the people he sent to the various rehab programs and kept me updated on their progress.

Six months later, in May, Darryl appeared at the mission, with his head resting in his hands, pretending to be asleep as he always used to do, though I knew he was awake. I tapped him on the shoulder, and said, "Hey Darryl! How are you? Did you finish the program?" He looked at me for a moment, then put his head back in his hands and ignored me. I sat down next to him and waited for him to speak. "You never finish the program Miss Donna" he said. "Tell me about that Darryl" I replied. "I failed. I relapsed, so I left" he said. I was sad but tried not to show my emotions. "Were you working?" I asked. "Yes, but I failed at that too since I relapsed." "Darryl," I asked, "Can you go back?" "Yes, but I don't know if I want to," he said." We had a short discussion, and I knew that Darryl was disappointed in himself and angry that he "failed" one more time. He had no idea what he planned on doing at this point, and the future was not even a thought. I told him that I was happy to see him and would try to get him back in the program if he wanted, but he just shook his head no. I reinforced that many people relapse, that he simply needed to try again, and that I believed in him. "Thanks" he said and put his head down and pretended to sleep; that was my cue to pat him on the shoulder and leave him alone for now. I knew the cure for Darryl: dream again. Unfortunately, when there are too many broken dreams, many people simply give up dreaming.

David was a very interesting man who I really liked but could never quite figure out. He was very polite, kind, and considerate, and always very neat and clean, even though he was homeless. He lived in a large shelter for men near the mission, though not affiliated with the mission. When he came for lunch, he would wipe down the chair before he sat down, even though we kept everything clean in the building. He did not drink or use drugs and was very intelligent. David told me he graduated from college with a degree in chemistry. He grew up in a small town about an hour away and had family still living there. When I asked why he would not go back home to be with his family, he simply laughed and said, "No, I can't do that." I never knew why… David came to the mission almost every day for lunch, and he was a regular at the Wednesday evening Steady Hands program. He was a Christian man who I know loved the Lord. After years of living at this men's shelter, David got a job there where he worked full time, so I did not see him anymore on a daily basis. He had some personal issues that he would come to talk to me about from time to time and we developed a good, trusting relationship. David had so much potential, and it frustrated me that he did not utilize his college degree and intelligence to make a life for himself where he was self-sufficient. He could have easily gotten a good job, an apartment, and perhaps even gotten married. He was charming, kind, honest, and good looking, but he did not see any of that in himself. He simply gave up on himself and was fearful of trying. I do not know what caused that fear, but it was powerful in his life and dominated his decisions. As far as I know, David remains at that shelter where I guess he may live out the rest of his life, though he was only in his early forties.

Paul was one of my favorite clients who I got to know fairly well. He was a regular for years and was one of the kindest and most intelligent clients I met in my six years at the mission. Paul was extremely well read, and always had a book of theology, religion, or philosophy in his backpack, and wanted to share ideas with me when he came to the mission. Paul was homeless by choice. He called himself a "free spirit" who could not be contained by four walls. He had a beautiful, deep voice, and sang when he played guitar, of which he played very well. He was around 50 years old, and in his youth, he played his guitar and sang in various bands. Paul loved his mother and called her "a saint." He frequently told me he thought she and I would be good friends if we ever met, and that we had a lot in common. He often tried to call her when he came to my office since he did not have a phone, and he had loving conversations with her, calling her "mommy" and always telling her that he loved her.

At one point in Paul's time at the mission we got him an apartment where he stayed for a few months, and he even got a job for a while. However, he said he felt guilty not paying any rent (a social program paid his rent for one year), so he laid the key to his apartment door on the kitchen counter and left. Paul told me he used drugs in his government-funded apartment, and also invited friends in to get high with him in his apartment. He said to me, "I know the government is not paying my rent so I can get high with friends, so I left." Paul was a heroin addict and alcoholic when he was younger but said he did not "fool around with that anymore." He did, however, use other drugs on a regular basis. Paul was so intelligent and talented, in addition to being so kind, that I really wanted to see him sober, housed, and working; he had so much potential.

After several years of knowing Paul, he came into my office and said he was finally ready to go (again) to rehab. He had gone so many times in the past and relapsed but told me after many of our conversations over the years that he was ready for a change. I was thrilled! We called his "mommy", and she was also very happy, but admitted to me that she was not sure he would stay since he had been in rehab so many times in the past. We all prayed together, and then I called Scott. In a few hours, Paul went to rehab, older, wiser, and more serious this time. He left me a beautiful letter in which he thanked me for my time over the years and for our many conversations and told me he had given his life to Christ and loved the Lord. I was hopeful.... A few weeks later, I saw Paul on the street and asked him what happened. He said he could not be confined to a building and a program and knew he would fail again at rehab, so he left and was back on the streets. I have not seen him since, but I do think of him from time to time

What happens when a very fragile, broken person, whose life has been extremely challenging, encounters yet another huge hurdle? One very disturbing prayer card I received in the prayer room was from Leslie. She wrote, "I am going through a bit of a struggle. I was brought up in church and I believe in God whole heartedly, but I've had a really bad life and it don't matter what way I turn, everything goes wrong. I grew up in foster care. When I was 18, I lost my mom and my kids, turned into an addict, and this summer lost my brother and sister, both 4 months apart. On Christmas Eve I had my 3rd stroke. I'm homeless and don't have no family. I don't have nobody, and I just need Him to see me one more time to hear me because He don't, and I can't push through no more. I'm tired and ready to give up." Wow... this was going to be a long conversation and I asked if we could have some future counseling sessions. I did, however, ask her at that time if she was suicidal, in which case we take clients to the hospital for immediate help. I asked her directly if she thought she might kill herself since she wrote that she was "ready to give up," but after asking the appropriate questions from my suicide intervention training (ASIST), about a plan, current and past substance abuse, past suicide attempts, etc., I believed her when she said she would not kill herself, and I felt comfortable setting up future appointments with her. I also recommended some mental health counselors for her to see in addition to the pastoral counseling that I would provide. In the past, I had called and made arrangements for other clients who were indeed suicidal and in immediate need of life-saving help. I saw Leslie a few more times after our initial meeting, and she sounded better, but then like so many other people who walk through the doors of a mission, she disappeared. The emotional energy needed to hear stories like this on a daily basis I admit, was exhausting.

Our building caught on fire in the early winter by a woman who was sleeping outside of the outreach center. She was lighting large pieces of cardboard from boxes to keep warm, and lit some boxes too close to the building, which caught fire. Fortunately, it was about 4:30 in the morning and no one was there. She inhaled a little of the smoke and was taken to the hospital but was otherwise unharmed. The mission staff and volunteers worked outside that day, never missing a days' work or lunch for our clients and continued to work outside for a couple of weeks until we were given a large, old building down the street (a former cultural center) to use until the Outreach Center was repaired. Only a small portion of this huge building was being used, so in exchange for rent, we fixed up some of the unused areas of this old building, while providing a warm and dry space for our clients to stay and to eat lunch.

One cold, wet day, a man named Joseph came to the cultural center in need of many things. I had never met Joseph before, and he said he was homeless and cold. He said he was hungry and that he needed some clothes and a coat. Joseph was a very large man, and I could not find anything that fit him, other than socks, a hat, and gloves, for which he thanked me. He ate lunch at our building and then asked if he could have a sleeping bag. The women who normally worked in our supply room were not there at the time, so I went in to find a sleeping bag. I gave him one (so I thought) and sent him off into the evening to try and stay warm, though I did strongly recommend some shelters for him to stay in that night. Joseph left, and I was very busy working that afternoon. Later that day when I went back into the supply room, I realized we were out of sleeping bags, and I gave him a tent instead, by mistake. I hoped Joseph would come back when he realized my mistake, but I never saw him again. I felt like I failed a client.

About six months later, after our original Outreach Center was repaired and now open, Joseph came for lunch. He asked if I was the chaplain, and I said yes. I did not immediately recognize him. He said, "I want to tell you an amazing story." Joseph then told me about my mistake (what I thought was a failure) in giving him a tent instead of a sleeping bag at the other building that last winter. I then, of course, remembered him and my failure and quickly apologized to him. I told Joseph that I recognized my mistake after he left that day and hoped he would return, but he did not. Joseph said that winter he froze outside in his tent, but had it not been for the tent which protected him from the cold rains, ice and snow, he might not have survived. He said he was so thankful for my mistake because he realized that he needed a tent more than a sleeping bag. Joseph was eventually moved into a motel for part of that winter by another one of our staff, but he was so grateful for the tent, even though he said he was very cold and thought he would surely die from hypothermia. God spared him in a miraculous way he said, and he wanted to tell me about his faith in God that stemmed from that cold winter and his tent. Joseph believed God divinely protected him and kept him from freezing to death, and he wanted to tell everyone about God's goodness, even to homeless people. He was also anxious to thank me for my mistake, or what I thought was my failure.

Maybe sometimes our failures are what God uses to show His love. Do not ever be afraid of making a mistake or failing if you at least try. Mother Teresa once wrote, "Allow God to use you without consulting you. Christ accepted death because He trusted His Father. He knew that from that apparent failure God will work out His plan of salvation. For us, too, we must have that deep faith and trust that if we are doing God's will, He will work out His plan of salvation in us and through us in spite of any failure we may meet" (Mother Teresa Center pamphlet).

One of the amazing ways God showed His love and worked out His plan of salvation was through one of my favorite characters in the Bible, the disciple Peter. Peter was sometimes impulsive and had a strong personality, and he also failed miserably. Most of us know the story of his betrayal to his friend, Lord, and Savior Jesus, after Jesus was arrested. All four gospels tell how Peter denied Jesus not once, but three times, but only the gospel of Luke says that Jesus was close enough to Peter to have perhaps heard his denial of Him as, "The Lord turned and looked at Peter" (Luke 22:61) after Peter's third denial in the courtyard. Can you imagine the horror Peter must have felt when his eyes and Jesus' eyes met? All four gospel accounts say that Peter "went out and wept bitterly" (Luke 22:62), knowing his utter betrayal and failure, yet he did not lose hope and quit.

After Jesus' resurrection, He approached Peter and asked Him three times if He loved Him. Jesus gave Peter three chances to affirm his love for Him, after denying Him three times. The gospel of John relays the loving conversation between Jesus and Peter, and Jesus never rebuked Peter or showed anger towards him for his failure. Instead, Jesus said, "*Follow me*" (John 21:19). Peter went on to become the leader of the Church and worked tirelessly spreading the Good News of Jesus Christ. Peter knew he had been mercifully forgiven and was able to put his failure behind him and move forward.

Understanding the nature of forgiveness is essential in getting past our failures and becoming the people God wants us to be. When we can forgive ourselves because we know God forgives us and will give us another chance, perhaps we too can forgive others who have harmed us. Fear of failure and the inability to understand, accept, or offer forgiveness can incapacitate people, cause people to give up, lose hope, and never achieve all God has planned for our lives. As a chaplain, teaching these concepts to people who have been homeless for many years and who may have done awful things in order to survive was quite challenging though, and could only be done through the powerful Words of the Bible, a lot of love, and the work of the Holy Spirit. I am reminded of the beautiful words of Mother Teresa who wrote,

> *"Love each other as God loves each of you, with an intense and particular love. Be kind to each other: It is better to commit faults with gentleness than to work miracles with unkindness"*

(Mother Teresa, No Greater Love, 20).

**The Bible is filled with very dysfunctional families,
sometimes followed by unbelievable
acts of forgiveness.**

3

The Need to Forgive

"We must develop and maintain the capacity to forgive. He who is devoid of the power to forgive is devoid of the power to love. There is some good in the worst of us and some evil in the best of us. When we discover this, we are less prone to hate our enemies." Dr. Martin Luther King Jr.

Working in the prayer room during walk-ins, I encountered all types of issues that I normally did not encounter in my daily life, which stretched my counseling skills, as well as my faith. One woman wrote on her prayer card, "My sister was murdered in 2019 and it's taking us so much to get all of this anger out. Please pray Jesus can give my family the strength we need." I was speechless for a moment when I read this woman's card, not so much because of the tragedy, but more so, because of her plea to Jesus to provide the strength the family needed to get through this terrible event. She did not speak of vengeance but instead reached out to God for help.

One man told me in the prayer room that his mentally challenged brother died of a heroin overdose. His "friends" dumped him out of their car in a hospital parking lot when he overdosed (while he was still alive) and left him to die alone in the middle of the night in the parking lot. Had this young man been taken into the hospital, his life might have been saved. After talking to my client about this horrible situation concerning his brother's death and inquiring about his faith, I asked if he thought he would ever be able to ever forgive the people who did this to his brother. "No" he understandably said. Compassion, non-judgement, and a listening ear was so needed, but I knew that until this man was able to forgive, he would carry this anger and bitterness for the rest of his life. He was not ready for a discussion on forgiveness, and I knew only the Holy Spirit would enable anyone to forgive such a tragedy, so I quietly listened and asked him if he wanted prayer, to which he said yes. I know Jesus said we must forgive our enemies, but I never had to deal with such an awful tragedy like this man, as well as the woman whose sister was murdered. Is the Christian life easy when God commands us to forgive? No, and I did not wish to pretend it is.

The tragic and awful stories these two people told me about in the prayer room reminded me of a story Corrie Ten Boom wrote about in several of her books concerning her own family during World War II in the concentration camps. Her family hid Jews in their home during the war and were caught and sent to the camps. Corrie Ten Boom was the only one in her family to survive the horrors of those concentration camps. Her book, *The Hiding Place,* recounts this terrible period in her life. I tell her story to people who want to forgive but have no idea how because it can be so difficult and humanly impossible without the grace of God.

Corrie Ten Boom wrote about impossible forgiveness when she was in a church in Munich, Germany and spoke to the people there about her and her family's experience in the concentration camps during World War II. In 1947 she traveled from Holland, her home country, to Germany with the message of God's forgiveness. She knew many of the German people felt guilty for the atrocities done to the Jewish people, and she wanted to express to them that God can forgive even the most heinous of sins when we turn to Him and ask Him.

After she finished speaking, Corrie Ten Boom stood in the back of the room to greet the people who came to hear her and she wrote, "And that's when I saw him, working his way forward against the others. One moment I saw the overcoat and the brown hat; the next, a blue uniform and a vizored cap with its skull and crossbones. It came back with a rush: the huge room with its harsh overhead lights, the pathetic pile of dresses and shoes in the centre of the floor, the shame of walking naked past this man. I could see my sister's frail form ahead of me, ribs sharp beneath the parchment skin. Betsie, how thin you were! Betsie and I had been arrested for concealing Jews in our home during the Nazi occupation of Holland; this man had been a guard at Ravensbruck concentration camp where we were sent" (Corrie Ten Boom, 76).

The old guard approached Corrie Ten Boom to greet her. He stood in front of her and put his hand out to shake hers. He told her that she gave a wonderful message, and he was so happy to hear that his sins were forgiven by a merciful God. Of course, this man did not remember her as one prisoner amongst thousands of other women. The guard said, "You mentioned Ravensbruck in your talk; I was a guard there… But since that time, I have become a Christian. I know that God has forgiven me for the cruel things I did there, but I would like to hear it from your lips as well" (Ten Boom, 76-77). Her sister Betsie died in the camp, and Corrie Ten Boom came face to face with the man partially responsible for Betsie's death, as well as her own suffering, and wondered how she could really forgive as God commands. She knew she had to forgive but shaking his hand and granting him her forgiveness was just too much to ask! But she wrote, "For I had to do it – I knew that. The message that God forgives has a prior condition: that we forgive those who have injured us. 'If you do not forgive men their trespasses,' Jesus said, 'neither will your Father in heaven forgive your trespasses'" (Ten Boom, 77). Corrie Ten Boom was of course referring to Matthew 6:14&15, which says, "*For if you forgive other people when they sin against you, your heavenly Father will also forgive you. But if you do not forgive others their sins, your Father will not forgive your sins."* For those of us who have suffered deep hurts and major injustices, yet love the Lord and claim to follow Him, do we really believe that Scripture concerning forgiveness and follow it, or do we merely glance over it without serious thought or stop to consider how it applies to our own lives?

When the war ended, Corrie Ten Boom had a home in Holland for victims of Nazi brutality. She wrote, "Those who were able to forgive their former enemies were able also to return to the outside world and rebuild their lives, no matter what the physical scars. Those who nursed bitterness remained invalids. It was as simple and as horrible as that" (Ten Boom, 77). She realized that forgiveness is not an emotion, something we feel like doing or not doing, but rather, forgiveness is an act of the will, and an act of obedience to God, so she prayed for Jesus to help her forgive this man. Corrie lifted her arm to shake his hand, and as she did, she said something amazing happened. "And so woodenly, mechanically, I thrust my hand into the one stretched out to me. And as I did, an incredible thing took place. The current started in my shoulder, raced down my arm, sprang into our joined hands. And then this healing warmth seemed to flood my whole being, bringing tears to my eyes. 'I forgive you brother!' I cried. 'With all my heart!' For a long moment we grasped each other's hands, the former guard and the former prisoner. I had never known God's love so intensely as I did then" (Ten Boom, 77-78).

The ability to forgive to the extent that Corrie Ten Boom forgave, I hope inspires all people to also forgive even the most cruel and hateful people as well, with the help of Jesus to whom she cried. Many people at the mission were astonished and deeply touched when I told this incredible story of forgiveness and they prayed for the Holy Spirit to allow them that same grace.

Some women I spoke with at the mission had been sexually abused as children by their fathers or their mother's boyfriends. Living with this horror often resulted in leaving home at an early age, bringing with them many emotional scars and no idea how to support themselves. In desperation and hunger, usually living alone on the streets at a young age, some of these women felt forced into prostitution; drug addiction soon followed. Several women told me their stories and said they wanted to change but did not know where to begin. Some of the women were abused by pimps of whom they were afraid to leave and felt trapped. Could they forgive the men who abused them as children, which led them into this nightmare of a life? No, they told me, they could not. I understood (to the extent that I was able), their reluctance and anger. Most of the women in these circumstances had no desire to forgive the men who abused them, but on rare occasions I would talk with women who wanted to forgive but said they did not know how; there was simply too much anger and hate. I would tell these women about Corrie Ten Boom's story, and they would often break down and cry. Forgiveness is possible through Christ.

I would provide spiritual counseling for any woman who wanted it, who lived such terrible lives as prostitutes and drug addicts and referred them for rehab and psychological counseling as well. We also took women to shelters where they could get away from their pimps and abusers and off the streets. The mission also opened a women's transitional house where women could get a fresh start. (I will speak more about this transitional house in a later chapter). Some of the women at our transitional house went back to school, some women got jobs or job training, and were able to live in a warm, loving, and safe environment, often for the first time in their lives. With mentoring, love, safety, and the Gospel, many women learned to forgive and break free from hatred and bitterness.

Some days I would see women come into the mission with bruises and black eyes. I would gently approach them to say hello and leave space to talk. Sometimes a woman in this condition would open up and ask if we could talk privately, but sometimes a woman hid her face and walked away. With little or no self-esteem, many of these women felt like they deserved the abuse they received from their significant others, their pimps, or their customers; in that situation, did they even think that forgiveness was necessary? For the women who knew they did not deserve the abuse they received but felt like they had nowhere else to go, forgiveness was pretty difficult. Only in Christ is anyone able to forgive the horrors too many people experience in this world. When we realize our own sinfulness and the fact that Jesus willingly forgives anyone who comes to Him, no matter how heinous the sin, only then can we ask the Holy Spirit to allow us to forgive the people who have damaged our lives and hurt us deeply. Once forgiveness takes place, lives can move forward, but without forgiveness, like Corrie ten Boom said, our lives remain crippled. I saw many crippled lives come and go at the mission.

My faith and Christian walk were stretched when a man came into the mission who several people told me was a pimp. This relatively young man was always well-dressed and always came in with a different woman, who I assumed was a prostitute since each woman was quiet and appeared almost subservient to him. He was rather rude and arrogant and spoke to these women in cruel and disrespectful ways. He would not let them out of his sight and they appeared to be unable to walk around the mission without him. Some of these women came to walk ins for some material items like food or clothing, but again, he would be right next to them. I wanted to talk to each of the various women he brought in alone, without him, to see if they would open up or ask for help, but I was never given that opportunity. I felt disgust and anger for this man, but I knew I had to treat him with kindness and show the love of Jesus to him, as I would to everyone else who came through the doors of the mission. Also, I could not confront him on hearsay, no matter how much I was told it was true. I also had to think about how God loves all of us and died for us, "while we were yet sinners" (Romans 5:8), which included me.

I have heard some people say that we are not obligated to forgive a person if they do not ask for our forgiveness, but is that biblical? I do not think so. While Jesus was literally being nailed to the Cross, He said, "Father, forgive them, for they know not what they do" (Luke 23:34). The men crucifying Jesus did not ask for His forgiveness at that time, but Jesus granted it anyway; should we not to do the same?

People who have not grown up surrounded by love and the concept of forgiveness obviously have a much harder time loving and forgiving others. Many years ago I had an amazing conversation with a hospice patient of mine when I worked as a hospice chaplain. Pat was an elderly woman whose husband was dying, and a couple of times a month I would visit them in their old wooden house deep in the Appalachian mountains of eastern Kentucky. One hot summer day I made a visit to this house that had no air conditioning, but Pat's husband Ken lay in his hospital bed in the living room and was cold. As his wife brought the blanket up around him, I noticed three fingers on her left hand were missing. Pat noticed that I looked at her hand and said to me, "It's hard sometimes with this hand. I got all my fingers blown off with a shotgun" she told me in a matter of fact manner. She pointed to her husband Ken and said, "His father shot at us with a shotgun and I put my hand up to close the door and protect us when I got my fingers blown away. He got hit in the neck; see the scar?" she asked as she pointed to his neck. "Tell me about this Pat, if you want to" I said. Pat went on to say, "Well, he just came after us with a shotgun, that's all" (as if this were normal I thought!). "Why?" I asked. "Oh, because his wife told him to; she said, 'shoot the SOB!' He was afraid of his wife, so he did whatever she told him. She was mean." I asked Pat if Ken was this woman's own son – her biological son, and she said yes. "What happened after that? Were you afraid? Did you call the police" I asked. I had many questions surrounding this unusual story! "No" Pat said. "They never came after us again. I was sure they wouldn't. Ken's father came to us later and asked for our forgiveness." "Did you forgive him?" I asked. Pat did not hesitate for a second and said, "Of course! I asked him if he asked the Lord for forgiveness, and he said he did, so if God could forgive him, then I must too." "Did Ken forgive his dad?" I asked. "Yes." "What about his mother who told his father to shoot him; did Ken forgive her?" Pat replied, "Oh, she never asked us for forgiveness, but we both forgave her. We actually didn't see her again until she was dying, and I held her hand until she died."

Obviously this was a very dysfunctional family, but Pat and Ken knew the love of the Lord and learned through the Bible and their church that forgiveness is not optional but is commanded by God. Can you imagine though, having your own parents shoot at you and try to kill you, and even more so, can you imagine forgiving them!?

The Bible is filled with very dysfunctional families, sometimes followed by unbelievable acts of forgiveness. A famous story in the Bible that deals with huge family problems and amazing forgiveness is the story of Joseph as recorded in Genesis chapters 37-50. Joseph was the favorite son of Jacob, who obviously did not hide that favoritism since his brothers were jealous of him. Genesis 37:3-4 says, *"Now Israel (Jacob) loved Joseph more than any other of his sons because he was the son of his old age. And he made him a robe of many colors. But when his brothers saw that their father loved him more than all of his brothers, they hated him and could not speak peacefully to him."*

One day Joseph's brothers were out in the fields tending their father's flock, and their father told Joseph to go out and check on his brothers. When they saw him approaching, they decided to kill him because of their jealousy. Joseph's brother Reuben did not want his brother killed, and another brother, Judah, thought it would be better to sell Joseph to some traders to at least make some money instead of killing him. The brothers agreed and sold Joseph to some Ishmaelites who were passing by for twenty shekels of silver. The Ishmaelites then sold Joseph to Potiphar (an officer of Pharoah) and he was taken to Egypt as a slave. Joseph's brothers told their father Jacob (Israel) that his youngest son Joseph had been killed by wild animals and was dead. Even though they saw that their father was extremely grief-stricken by this news, they never told him the truth and allowed their own father to mourn for many years, thinking that his favorite son Joseph was dead.

Joseph found great favor with Potiphar and was made overseer of his entire house. Potiphar trusted Joseph to manage everything within his household and had great respect for Joseph. Potiphar's wife thought Joseph was very handsome and wanted to sleep with him, but he refused her advances. Joseph told his master's wife, *"Because of me my master has no concern about anything in the house, and he has put everything that he has in my charge. He is not greater in this house than I am, nor has he kept anything back from me except you, because you are his wife. How then can I do this great wickedness and sin against God?"* Eventually his master's wife got tired of being turned down by Joseph and lied about him, telling her husband that he tried to rape her. His master threw him in jail. Joseph still trusted God, despite all of these horrible events in his life, and was eventually even put in charge of the other prisoners!

While in prison, Joseph correctly interpreted some difficult dreams of two of his fellow prisoners, Pharoah's baker and his cupbearer. They were both released, though the baker was killed, which Joseph predicted from the dream. Two years later, Pharoah had a dream that he could not understand and which greatly troubled him. Pharoah's cupbearer remembered that Joseph interpreted his dream correctly while in prison and told Pharoah that he thought Joseph could therefore interpret Pharoah's dream as well. So Joseph was brought up from the prison and did indeed interpret Pharoah's dream concerning seven years of good crops followed by seven years of famine. Pharoah was so impressed with Joseph that he released him from the prison and eventually put him in charge of all of the food in Egypt to prepare for the future famine. Joseph was made second in command in all of Egypt, second only to Pharoah himself.

When the famine did come and spread all over the land, Egypt was the only country in the area that had food since Joseph had stockpiled the crops to sell to the surrounding countries. Joseph's father and brothers were living in the land of Canaan and heard that there was food in Egypt, so Joseph sent his sons to Egypt to buy some food so they would not starve. Joseph was the governor of Egypt and in charge of food distributions. One day he saw his brothers come to him for food, though they did not recognize him. How many of us would refuse them food after what they did to him? How many of us would let our family know how great and powerful we became since being sold by our brothers? But Joseph did not do either of those things. He did not disclose his identity and he sold them large portions of food. He even returned their money and hid it in their sacks of food! Joseph asked his brothers many questions about his family. He asked if his father was still alive (which he was) and about his brother Benjamin, who was not with them.

The story of Joseph and his family is found throughout many chapters in Genesis, but the story ends with Joseph eventually revealing himself to his brothers and then forgiving them for what they did to him. Joseph even asked Pharoah if his brothers and father could come to Egypt to live and he provided very generously for them all. He held no grudge and felt no hatred for his brothers who did such an evil thing to him years ago. Joseph's forgiveness is an act that not many people would do after suffering so much for so many years. Even though Joseph obviously came from a dysfunctional family, by God's grace, he was able to overcome the pain caused by his own brothers, and even showed them great love and generosity.

Most of the people who come through the doors of a rescue mission are from very dysfunctional families where love was often absent. However, if the staff and volunteers of a Gospel mission can love them and also show them the love and forgiveness of Christ, they too can learn to forgive heinous events that have happened to them as well, just like Corrie Ten Boom, Pat and Ken, and Joseph. If a person is loved, surrounded by loving people, and especially if they learn about and experience the sacrificial love of Jesus, then yes, forgiveness is indeed possible.

As the chaplain, I heard so many heart-breaking stories of abuse, neglect, violence, and abandonment, stories the average person simply does not hear or experience. Broken people generally come from very broken homes and they simply need to be put back together again by a loving Savior who most of our clients have never known. What a wonderful opportunity it is to love and forgive the unloved and teach them about the love and forgiveness of Jesus; that is how lives change.

There is one amazing act of forgiveness that occurred within the mission that involved Jim, the Executive Director, and a client named Alexander. One day, after hours when the mission was closed, Alexander (a regular client) was hanging out near the mission. He heard a sound like a door banging back and forth in the wind and went to investigate. Alexander said he found the back door of the mission partially open and went inside. He roamed around the building and said he found a hat that looked like something his mother would wear when she was young and he became very nostalgic, thinking about her. He also found a necklace that he picked up that he thought was pretty which also reminded him of his mom. Alexander said he had no intention of stealing anything or doing any damage to the mission, but he thought he might look around to see if he could find some clothes to keep warm since he was homeless, and maybe some food since he was hungry.

The security system alerted Jim (the executive director of the mission), that someone had entered the building after hours, so he decided to check it out for himself rather than call the police to come. Jim expected it to be another false alarm, which occurred on occasion. However, once Jim unlocked the front door and began (bravely, I think) searching the building, he found Alexander in the restroom in the back of the outreach center with a few food items with him from the pantry. He told

Jim that he did not break in but entered through the back door, which had not been securely shut. Jim sat down with Alexander and asked who he was and what he was doing there, and he appeared to be very honest and non-threatening. He also told Jim that he had previously received some valuable help from the mission staff for which he appreciated. There had been no harm done as far as Jim could tell, so he called the police to come and make a report. Jim (surprisingly) told the police that he was not going to press charges and then warned Alexander not to do this again, or he might have to take more serious action. Alexander seemed very appreciative of Jim's treatment of him, and he departed.

Jim loved the mission and the clients who we serve and he treated Alexander with kindness and with the love of a forgiving Savior. When I heard about what occurred that day, I was surprised, but not shocked since I knew Jim's heart; after all, he is the man who started the mission with his wife Becky. I spoke with Alexander later about this incident, and he said he was embarrassed about it and was not thinking clearly. We had a good conversation about forgiveness people like Jim give because of the forgiveness Jesus grants to us. Alexander knows the Bible and he and I often discussed Scripture, but drugs had a hold on him that prevented his life from moving forward.

When I spoke to Alexander about the forgiveness Jim granted him, we also discussed the forgiveness God grants us. We are all underserving of God's mercy, but because of His love for us, He willingly died for our sins to forgive us and to bring us back into a relationship with Him. Alexander understands that love, and in my last conversation with him he said that someday he wants to get baptized and live in the reality of that amazing forgiveness; I pray that day comes soon, and I pray I can be the one to baptize him.

**God's mercy reaches farther than any of us
can begin to comprehend.**

4

When We Know Better

"For all have sinned and fall short of the glory of God"
Romans 3:23

There I was, hanging upside down like a bat with my ankle
stuck in-between the rungs of a tall extension ladder, utterly
helpless and in a great deal of pain. My leg started shaking with
the pain as I stared at the unbelievable predicament of which I
found myself. I was in my backyard one morning painting my
gazebo. There is a ball on the very top of the gazebo roof that
was in much need of paint since most of the previous paint
was worn off and the wood was now beginning to rot. I had
worked as a professional painter for over twenty years prior to
becoming a chaplain, and I knew this ball could be painted, but
the ladder set-up and reach would be difficult due to the steep
pitch of the gazebo roof. I set up my extension ladder at a large
angle, digging it firmly into the grass so it would not slip, and
up I went. I had most of my weight on my right leg, which was
on the roof, and stepped lightly with my left leg on the ladder
(that rested against the gazebo) as I reached as far as I could to
paint this ball.

I safely completed painting the ball on the roof, climbed
down the ladder, and began painting the facia boards and the
lattice of the gazebo. Looking back at the ball on top, I figured it
needed another coat since the wood was dry, so I climbed back
up the ladder for the second coat. After several ladder moves, I
was just about done and saw one small area that needed some
paint. Not wanting to climb down and wrestle with moving the
ladder through the tree branches for that final move, I put my
left foot on the rung of the extension ladder that was not resting

on the gazebo, but which extended into the air, even though I knew that was a stupid thing to do since that is not safe; I just wanted to paint that final spot. I immediately remembered my many ladder safety lessons from Trade school many years ago, that said to never step on the rung of a ladder that was not resting on any surface. I thought most of my weight was on my other leg standing on the roof, so for just a second I would be fine. I knew better... in a split second, the top of the ladder slid down and trapped my ankle like a vice, throwing me backwards and left me hanging upside down like a bat. As I hung there, I deeply regretted doing something I knew I should not have done - yet did it anyway.

Hanging from the ladder, knowing I was alone and did not have my phone nearby, I strategized about how to get out of this rather dangerous predicament. Maybe if I could get my shoe off I could slide my foot out from between the rungs and slide my body down. I pulled my body up enough to untie and remove my shoe, but to no avail; I still could not slip my foot out. Now, the ladder simply crushed my foot instead of my shoe! I desperately tried to push the ladder up, but the weight of my body hanging down prevented the ladder from moving. I was angry at myself and felt awfully stupid for having done such a foolish thing. Knowing I looked quite crazy hanging from this ladder, but unable to break free, I started to yell, "Help! Anyone! Please help me!" It was a hot August afternoon, and the neighbors were either at work or inside their air-conditioned homes. We also have a tall wooden privacy fence around our back yard so no one could see me, of which a part of me in my pride, was relieved. My husband would not be home from work for hours and I began to panic. I looked down at the ground below me to see if there was anything I might smash my head on whenever I fell. Fortunately, I was hanging over grass, so at least the fall would not be so hard. I found a tree branch hanging just above my head, so I grabbed onto it, prayed it would not snap, and forcefully swung on it, twisting my body enough to turn the top of the ladder over and off of the gazebo in order to crash-land the ladder (I know this sounds rather stupid, but I figured that would be the only way I could release my foot). The bucket of paint I had hooked onto the ladder went flying, along with the ladder with me on it, and I hit the ground with a violent thud. I finally broke my foot free from the rungs of the ladder, rolled over and got up. I could barely breathe from the hard fall onto my side, and my ankle and foot were throbbing. My shins and ankle were cut, but I was able to walk. Hopefully nothing on my body was broken except for a few cracked ribs as I looked at the crushed paint can, that could have been my head. I limped into the house, half crying, half angry, half breathing, shocked at what just transpired. I got myself into a real mess that could have turned out much worse and changed my life forever. What if I broke my neck and became paralyzed? I was so thankful to God for saving me and sparing me from what could have easily been a life-changing event, even when I knew better...

My accident caused me to think about some of the clients at the mission, and the grave mistakes they made in the past that changed their lives, often times knowing better, but making the mistakes anyway. I spoke to many clients who in the past had houses, loving families, good jobs, nice cars, and lost it all because of one simple and foolish action that forever changed their lives, and the lives of their loved ones.

Sometimes people make many poor decisions and do things they know they should not do but do not seem to suffer any real consequences, like me and the ladder accident. However, like many of the clients I spoke with, it might only take that one wrong decision to forever alter the course of a life or lives. But let's not be judgmental. We have all made mistakes when we knew better; sometimes we "get away with it," but sometimes our poor decisions alter the course of our lives forever. What about having a little too much to drink and knowing you should not drive home but did it anyway? The result? Maybe a DUI and jail, or worse, killing your passenger or another driver and a long prison sentence. Regret forever. What about marrying that person who you knew was unreasonable and violent, but thought maybe you might change them and married them anyway, only to find yourself a victim of physical and emotional abuse? Or perhaps your children are now in danger and abused by your spouse. What about that decision to join a gang, knowing you should not get involved, but did so anyway because you longed for acceptance? Then, out of fear, you were forced to do things you knew you should not do but did them anyway and ended up in jail. What about that time you stole something, knowing you should not steal, yet you did it anyway, and got caught? Now as a person sits in jail, they regret doing what they knew they should not have done. Maybe it was that pressure or curiosity about taking some drug, knowing it was highly addictive, but did it anyway, and now you are an addict.

How many things have people done, when they knew better and realized they should not have done it, but did it anyway, and their lives have been forever changed? After having a criminal record, how have their relationships changed with their families? Their friends? How has a criminal record affected their employment opportunities? Their finances? What have many people lost in this life that could have been prevented, by doing something they knew they should not do, yet did it anyway?

On the other hand, like me stepping onto that ladder where I knew I should not have stepped, how often has God spared us from disaster when we did something we knew we should not have done, yet did it anyway? God's mercy reaches farther than any of us can begin to comprehend. I am sure you can think of some events in your own life where you knowingly made big mistakes or used poor judgment, yet God spared you from some terrible consequences. I pray we are all thankful for God's protection over us when we do not deserve it. While my stepping onto the wrong rung of a ladder was obviously not a sin but rather just a stupid mistake and poor judgment, it reminds me of "mistakes" and poor judgments that truly are sins, and which have very bad consequences.

In the Bible, there are numerous examples of people doing things they knew they should not do, but did them anyway, which altered their lives, the lives of their families, and even life in the entire world. Let's start at the beginning, in the book of Genesis. Most of us know the story of Adam and Eve, the first humans God created. God created everything good for them, and placed them in a beautiful garden, The Garden of Eden, to work it and keep it. *"And the Lord God commanded the man, saying, 'You may surely eat of every tree of the garden, but of the tree of the knowledge of good and evil you shall not eat, for in that day that you eat of it you shall surely die'"* (Genesis 2:16-17). We also know the story in Genesis chapter three when Adam and Eve knew better but went ahead and ate from the forbidden tree anyway.

"Now the serpent was more crafty than any other beast of the field that the Lord God had made. He said to the woman, 'Did God actually say, you shall not eat of any tree in the garden?' And the woman said to the serpent, 'We may eat of the fruit of the trees of the garden, but God said, 'You shall not eat of the tree that is in the midst of the garden, neither shall you touch it, lest you die.' But the serpent said to the woman, 'You will not

surely die. For God knows that when you eat of it your eyes will be opened, and you will be like God, knowing good and evil.' So when the woman saw the tree was good for food, and that it was a delight to the eyes, and that the tree was to be desired to make one wise, she took of the fruit and ate, and also gave some to her husband who was with her, and he ate. Then the eyes of both were opened, and they knew that they were naked" (Genesis 3:1-7).

Obviously Adam had told Eve that God forbade them from eating of the one tree, since she told Satan they were not allowed to eat of it, and obviously Adam was standing near Eve when Satan approached her and asked about the fruit, since after she ate, Scripture says that Eve gave some of the fruit to Adam, *"who was with her."* Next God comes back onto the scene and asks why they were hiding and how they knew they were naked. *"But the Lord God called to the man and said to him, 'Where are you?' And he said, 'I heard the sound of you in the garden, and I was afraid, because I was naked and I hid myself'. He said, 'Who told you that you were naked? Have you eaten of the tree of which I commanded you not to eat?' The man said, 'The woman you gave to be with me, she gave me the fruit of the tree, and I ate it.' Then the Lord God said to the woman, 'What is this you have done?' The woman said, 'The serpent deceived me and I ate'"* (Genesis 3:9-13). Adam and Eve both blamed someone other than themselves because they knew better but went ahead and did what they knew was wrong anyway.

Unfortunately, this first man and woman were not the only ones who suffered the consequences for their huge mistake, but all of the earth and every subsequent person on the earth would also suffer the consequences. There were probably so many beautiful trees to eat of in the garden, yet they made that choice to eat from the only one they were told not to eat of and brought on the destruction of everything. In their desire for wisdom and the power to "be like God" as the serpent told them, they did something they should not have done, even though they knew better...

Another well-known example in the Bible comes out of the book of Exodus. Moses had recently led the Israelites out of slavery in Egypt and they were all on their way to the Promised Land. God called Moses up to Mount Sinai to speak with him and give him the Ten Commandments for the people to live by, "*When the people saw that Moses delayed to come down from the mountain, the people gathered themselves together to Aaron and said to him, 'Up, make gods who shall go before us. As for this Moses, the man who brought us up out of the land of Egypt, we do not know what has become of him.' So Aaron said, to them 'Take off the rings of gold that are in the ears of your wives, your sons, and your daughters, and bring them to me.' So all the people took off their rings of gold that were in their ears and brought them to Aaron. And he received the gold from their hand and fashioned it with a graving tool and made a golden calf. And they said, 'These are your gods, O Israel, who brought you out of the land of Egypt!' And when Aaron saw this, he built an altar before it.*" (Exodus 32:1-5a).

God then instructed Moses to go down from the mountain and see what the people were doing, worshipping and sacrificing to their new god, the golden calf (Exodus 32:8). Moses was shocked and enraged. "*And Moses said to Aaron, 'What did this people do that you have brought such a great sin upon them?' And Aaron said, 'Let not the anger of my lord burn hot. You know the people, that they are set on evil. For they said to me, 'Make us gods who shall go before us. As for Moses, the man who brought us up out of the land of Egypt, we do not know what has become of him.' So I said to them, 'Let any who have gold take it off.' So they gave it to me, and I threw it in the fire, and out came this calf'"* (Exodus 32:21-24).

Like Adam and Eve, Aaron knew he did something terribly wrong, blamed others, made up a ridiculous excuse, yet he still made the terrible mistake anyway. The result of this "mistake," rather this sin, was the death of about three thousand men (Exodus 32:28). Perhaps Aaron feared the people and maybe even doubted God, wondering where Moses was himself, and cost the lives of thousands of men. Aaron knew better than to make that golden calf, yet he did so anyway...

Another famous example of using terrible judgment and making a huge mistake when he knew better was King David. David was Israel's greatest king and he was called a *"man after God's own heart"* and *"a man who will do God's will"* (1 Samuel 13:14 and Acts 13:22). David knew the Ten Commandments, including the commandment, *"You shall not commit adultery"* (Exodus 20:14). Yet here we find King David tempted by a beautiful woman, Bathsheba, of whom he was told was married to Uriah the Hittite (2 Samuel 11:3). David sent one of his soldiers to get her and he committed adultery with her, knowing it was a sin, but went ahead and did it anyway. David tried to hide his sin, but to no avail. Bathsheba informed him that she became pregnant, so now he was desperate and knew had to do something else that was a sin; he had her husband killed on the front lines of the war and then had Bathsheba brought to his home, married her, and hoped no one would have known about his adultery.

However, in 2 Samuel chapter 12, the king was confronted by a man named Nathan who told David a story about a rich man who had many flocks of sheep, yet he took the one beloved little ewe lamb from a poor man and had it killed and served it for a dinner, which devastated this poor man since he loved his only lamb as if it were his own child. Enraged, David said, "'*As the Lord lives, the man who has done this deserves to die, and he shall restore the lamb fourfold because he did this thing, and because he had no pity.' Nathan said to David, 'You are the man'...David said to Nathan, 'I have sinned against the Lord*" (2 Samuel 5-7a & 13a).

As a result of this sin, this huge mistake and lack of judgment on David's part, Nathan prophesied and told David that God said "*Now therefore the sword shall never depart from your house, because you have despised me and taken the wife of Uriah the Hittite to be your wife. Thus says the Lord, 'Behold, I will raise up evil against you out of your own house. And I will take your wives before your eyes and give them to your neighbor, and he shall lie with your wives in the sight of this sun. For you did it secretly, but I will do this thing before all Israel and before the sun.' David said to Nathan, 'I have sinned against the Lord.' And Nathan said to David, 'The Lord also has put away your sin; you shall not die. Nevertheless, because by this deed you have utterly scorned the Lord, the child born to you shall die*'" (2 Samuel 12:10-14). The child did indeed die, and through the years, David had many problems within his own family, including a son who tried to kill him and take over the throne, and a daughter who was raped. Evil did indeed come out of David's own house for many years, and a lot of people suffered as a result of one man who through his uncontrolled lust, did something very wrong, even though he knew better...

Let's go to the New Testament for a couple of more examples of people who knew they should not do something but went ahead and did it anyway. We will start with one man who everyone knows – Judas. Judas was one of Jesus' twelve disciples, who Jesus even called His friend (Matthew 26:50). Judas was paid thirty pieces of silver to betray Jesus and bring

Him into the hands of His enemies. Judas had traveled with Jesus for three years and heard Him preach. He had witnessed Jesus' acts of healing, mercy, love and compassion. Judas knew Jesus was no threat to Rome or to anyone. Yet out of greed, Judas betrayed his friend Jesus, even though he knew better.

The gospel of Matthew says, "*When morning came, all the chief priests and elders of the people took counsel against Jesus to put him to death. And they bound him and led him away and delivered him over to Pilate the governor. Then when Judas, his betrayer, saw that Jesus was condemned, he changed his mind and brought back the thirty pieces of silver to the chief priests and the elders, saying, 'I have sinned by betraying innocent blood.' They said, 'What is that to us? See to it yourself.' And throwing down the pieces of silver into the temple, he departed and went and hanged himself*" (Matthew 27:1-5). Judas knew better. He knew Jesus was innocent, yet out of greed, perhaps even jealousy, for one brief moment, Judas made the decision to do something he knew he should not have done, yet did it anyway, which caused the torture and death of the Son of God.

And then there is the disciple Peter. Peter loved Jesus and believed in Him, but he was also so sure of himself. After Jesus instituted the Lord's Supper at the Passover meal, He and His disciples went out to the Mount of Olives where Jesus told them, "*You will all fall away because of me this night. For it is written, 'I will strike the shepherd, and the sheep of the flock will be scattered.' But after I am raised up, I will go before you to Galilee.' Peter answered him, 'Though they all fall away because of you, I will never fall away.' Jesus said to him, 'Truly I tell you, this very night, before the rooster crows, you will deny me three times.' Peter said to him, 'Even if I must die with you, I will not deny you!*'" (Matthew 26:31-35).

Later that same night, when Jesus was led away in chains and delivered over to Pilate for crucifixion, Peter followed the crowd into the courtyard to hear what was going on and what would be the fate of Jesus. Just as Jesus had previously told Peter, three separate people said they recognized Peter as being with Jesus and that he had the same accent, and three separate times, Peter denied even knowing Jesus; then the rooster crowed. Peter, out of fear for his own safety and life, lied and betrayed his friend Jesus, knowing it was wrong yet did it anyway, *"And he went out and wept bitterly"* (Matthew 26:75b). If we are wise, we will recognize our mistakes, our sins, our lack of judgment, and then repent and become stronger people like Peter, who, after Jesus' resurrection, fearlessly preached the Gospel until his own martyrdom.

There are many stories of people who come to the mission who did things they knew they should not do but did them anyway, for a number of reasons. Vicky gave me one example of making a poor choice when she knew better. Vicki comes to the mission almost every day and attends chapel and Steady Hands when she is able. Years ago, she was married for many years, but then her husband left her. Vicki wondered what made her husband leave and why she was not loved. They got back together for a while, but he then left again and moved in with another woman. Vicki, of course, was crushed, and through a series of events after their divorce she became homeless. A family member gave her money for a hotel, and she soon met a man (who appeared to love her) who she invited to stay with her at the hotel. Vicki said she knew that she should not get involved with this man, especially since he was a drug addict, but because she felt hurt, unloved, and lonely, she continued with the relationship for several years. At that time, and in retrospect, she knew she should not have been in this relationship, but out of the basic human desire to feel love, she went ahead anyway, even when she knew better. Nothing good came out of that unhealthy relationship. So many poor choices and sins are committed because of our desire for love, even when we know it falls outside of God's parameters. Vicki is older and wiser today and loves the Lord. After attending chapel services at the mission for a few years she decided to get baptized. She continues to grow in her faith as she comes to the mission every day to hear the Word of God and embrace His love for her. She is also most grateful for the love she feels from the staff and volunteers at the mission, and she now understands that she is indeed loved by so many people, and of course, by God.

There are many examples in the Bible and at the mission of people who did the wrong thing, when they knew better, yet went ahead anyway. Think of some examples in your own life; we all have some. Are you not immeasurably grateful for such a loving God who forgives us and gives us second, sometimes third and fourth chances? So often, people, out of fear, lust, jealousy, greed, loneliness, or a longing for love and acceptance, do things they know they should not do, yet do them anyway, and then find themselves in their current predicaments. May we pray for the ability to show God's grace and mercy to those people who are indeed suffering the consequences of their mistakes, and remember that, there but for the grace of God, go I.

5

Lost in This World

"For the Son of Man came to seek and to save the lost"
Luke 19:10

The late Trappist monk Thomas Merton once wrote that being a monk reminded him of "Who God is – that we may get sick of the sight of ourselves and turn to Him: in the end, we will find Him in ourselves, in our own peaceful natures which have become the mirror of His tremendous Goodness and of His endless love" (Merton, 410). What would make someone sick of themselves? What finally causes some people to turn to God and through the power of His Holy Spirit, begin the sanctification process that causes them to be more like Christ and understand His endless love? Helping people recognize that the despair they feel in their lives because of their current situation can be changed is a large part of working at a rescue mission, especially for a chaplain. Many of the core changes that are needed begin with spiritual issues.

Most of the people who come through the doors of a mission are indeed lost in the world and do not feel they have any meaningful role in society, and in all honesty, most currently do not. Fortunately, we have a God who loves all people, and He made us in His image with the potential to love and serve Him, and to live meaningful lives. In his book *The Ragamuffin Gospel*, Brennan Manning wrote, "The Ragamuffin Gospel was written for the bedraggled, beat-up, and burnt-out. It is for the sorely burdened who are still shifting the heavy suitcase from one hand to the other. It is for the wobbly and the weak-kneed who know they don't have it all together and are too proud to accept the handout of amazing grace. It is for the inconsistent, unsteady disciples whose cheese is falling off their cracker. It is for the poor, weak, sinful men and women with hereditary faults and limited talents. It is for the earthen vessels who shuffle along on feet of clay. It is for the bent and the bruised who feel that their lives are a grave disappointment to God. It is for smart people who know they are stupid and honest disciples who admit they are scalawags. The Ragamuffin Gospel is a book I wrote for myself and anyone who has grown weary and discouraged along the Way." (Manning, no page numbers given). Manning described the majority of our clients.

I met quite a few people at the mission who had no ambitions, no dreams for a better life, no desire for rehab and sobriety, and were content "existing" each day and hanging out at the mission. Some of these same people often bragged about the good meals they could find in the dumpsters every evening when pizza places and other restaurants closed and had to throw out the leftover food from the day. They were happy to get this "good food" from the dumpsters since they were able to share it with others in their homeless camps, of which they all appreciated. The desire for community, acceptance, and love is strong.

How do people get so discouraged and lost in this world? Often, it stems from one's upbringing and family life, or more often, lack of a family life. One young man, Matt, came to my office one day and told me that he had uncontrollable "bad thoughts" that continued to run through his head, and thought he was going crazy. When I asked him for an example of a "bad thought" he would not give me one, but he did tell me he was dealing with the death of a close family member. Having formerly worked as a hospice chaplain and grief counselor for many years, I told him his "bad "thoughts might simply be part of his grief, and that perhaps he might want to focus on dealing with the death of this family member and the grief he was feeling from this loss. Matt did not agree with me and resisted anything I suggested. When I asked this young man about his ideas and belief about God, people, the world, pretty much about anything surrounding his world view, he said he believed "in nothing." When you are closed to any type of belief system, especially a belief in God, perhaps it is easy to get lost in the world.

One belief system I (thankfully) did not often encounter at the mission was the belief and practice of evil, such as witchcraft and devil worship, which was very unsettling. One day during walk-ins a young woman came in with an older man, who both made me feel very uncomfortable; I felt an evil and unsettling presence around them. I invited them into our hospitality room and asked them to fill out the paper we give to each client so they could write down who they are what they need. The man said he did not need anything but brought "his friend" here for some help. This woman did not speak very much and said she had to use the bathroom, so I showed her where it was (across from the hospitality room) and returned to a very busy and crowded room of clients. Instead of going into the bathroom, the woman sat outside of the door, rocking back and forth in a fetal position. Her male friend went outside to smoke. I went over and sat on the floor next to the woman and tried to ascertain what was going on with her. I wanted to get her off the floor and into the hospitality room for help, or to a private room if she desired, and figure out what was going on with her. I finally managed to get her off the floor and started to take her into a private room, when I saw her friend walk back down the hall.

This particular day was a very busy, hectic, and crowded day with many clients in need, and as I walked back towards my office, I saw a pile of feces on the floor in front of the bathroom door. Did this woman move her bowels on the floor instead of in the bathroom, which she never went into? I was quite shocked. I said something to the other clients about not going near the bathroom until we get something to clean up the waste, and the male friend said, "That's o.k. I'll get it" and with a bare hand, bent down to pick it up. My boss walked down the hall at this moment, and we both said to the man, "Wait!" However, he proceeded to pick up the feces with his bare hand, while my boss and I both turned around in disgust, unable to watch. The man laughed and said, "Look, its fake!" I thought how childish this gross prank was, coming from a middle-aged man at a Gospel Mission. With a crowded room full of clients and this woman in need (who seemed totally oblivious as to what just happened with this fake feces), there was no time to do anything but quickly compose myself from this gross shock. I now knew that perhaps more than I initially realized, this woman needed help.

I took the woman to my office, which also served as the prayer room, motioned for her to sit down, and asked what was going on in her life. She said she did not really know this man that she came in with but had been staying at a hotel with him for the last few days. She did not want to go back with him that evening and said she was afraid. I asked her if she wanted prayer, but she said no. She then mumbled something about witches, but I could not understand what she was saying. She also appeared to be under the influence of some drug. Her body continued to rock back and forth. I was a little nervous and began silently praying for God's protection. I called in another staff person so as not to be alone with this woman, in addition to opening the door which I had previously closed for privacy. After further questions and a disjointed and confusing discussion with this woman, I spoke to my boss for advice on what to do for this seemingly spiritually and emotionally tortured woman. My boss told me to go to the resource counselor, who then made a phone call to a woman's domestic abuse shelter; they told us to bring her over. Another mission worker and I told the woman we would take her to this shelter where she would be safe; she was hesitant but agreed to go. My co-worker pulled up the mission van, and we asked her to get in. Her male friend followed us outside and asked where we were taking her, but of course we did not tell him, but simply said she needed some help. "She sure does" he said, though he was still insistent on knowing where we were going; we would not disclose that information.

My co-worker drove, while I kept my eye on this woman who continued to rock back and forth in the back seat of the van. She then said that she was a witch and practiced witchcraft. No wonder I had an uneasy feeling around her. She said she worshipped the devil and spoke about witch covens that she attended and the sexual "sacrifices" that were made at these events. She made very confusing and jumbled statements about rape and sodomy, and then rocked her body faster and faster. Part of me feared for our own safety, not knowing what this woman might try to do. I continued to silently pray – and watch her. I started to think that maybe this shelter was not the best place to take her, but we continued our drive. We drove into the country for about 20 or 30 minutes until we got to the locked gate of this beautiful property. We pushed the button on the gate to talk to someone inside, and when they answered, we told them who we were. They had of course expected us and opened the gate for our entry. I spoke to the director of this shelter in private and told her about the witchcraft and probable drug use, and if there was perhaps some other more appropriate place we should take her to instead. The director thanked me for the information and said they would handle things from there. We offered any additional help if they needed, of which they thanked us, and we left. I never found out what happened to this poor woman, and I never saw her male friend again. Going down a path of devil worship and witchcraft is a sure way to get lost in the world. Here in America, we sometimes forget that "*we do not wrestle against flesh and blood, but against the rulers, against the authorities, against the cosmic powers over this present darkness, against the spiritual forces of evil in the heavenly places*" (Ephesians 6:12).

Another man, Rich, suffered from PTSD. He said he had been a train conductor for years and hit several men during his career who stood or sat on the train tracks in order to kill themselves. Rich said by the time he saw these various men on the tracks, he was unable to stop the train and unfortunately ended up killing them. Angrily, he said to me, "You can't stop a huge train in time to prevent hitting these fools!" He became quite angry as he spoke about these past horrors and told me he simply could not get the images of their deaths out of his mind. He used drugs to deaden these memories.

Many combat veterans also fall into this same cycle of drug abuse in their vain attempts to erase the memories and images that stick in their minds, and of the horrible acts they committed during war. I encountered a great deal of PTSD in combat veterans when I worked in a Veterans Administration hospital years ago, as well as with veterans who came to the mission. "Why don't they get help?" some people have asked me. Well, some do go for help such as counseling, but it does not always help them in the manner or speed they desire. Others simply do not know of the resources available to them, while others think they can handle their painful memories on their own and view seeking help as a weakness. Drug use often becomes their means of escape.

Illegal drug use and addictions are probably the biggest reason people's lives fall apart and they get so lost. A large percentage of the people who come to our mission deal with addiction issues. I met a couple of men during my time at the mission who were "carnies," the people who travel the country and work at carnivals. One carnie named Chris said he estimated that 99% of carnival workers have a drug habit to support. I do not know if that number is accurate or not, but after being a carnival worker for many years, that is what Chris believed to be true. He told me a story about when a carnival came to town years ago and he approached the boss of the carnival. He told him, "I have no money. I have a habit that I have to support, and I need a job." The boss told him he would hire him if his habit did not get in the way of his work and it did not get anyone hurt through negligence and being high. (I must say, I now think twice about going to carnivals)! Carnival workers get free meals, make an average of about $4.00 an hour, and work 50-60 hours a week, paid in cash, which comes to about $250.00 a week. However, the day they arrive at a town and set up and the day they leave and tear everything down is typically a 16-hour workday. Usually there is someone working at the carnival who sells drugs, making it easy for workers to keep up their habit.

Instead of working a transient, seasonal job for very low pay and easy access to drugs like a carnival, the mission has an employment program that helps lost people find self-respect by becoming self-sufficient through stable work. The staff who work in the employment area of the mission also teach a "Jobs For Life" class to help their clients prepare for the work force. This class is a 16 week course with a biblical foundation. Jobs For Life focuses on working in general, conflict resolution, and emotional and physical roadblocks clients deal with and how those roadblocks might affect stable employment. The class also focuses on individual characteristics and the talents and gifts each student possesses and how those talents can be utilized for various types of work. The employment program at the mission also gives clients appropriate clothing to wear on their job interviews, teaches them how to conduct themselves in a job interview, and then assists people in finding gainful employment which is available for anyone who comes to the mission if they want it; the main challenge is getting clients to want to work and to take pride in being self-sufficient and independent.

One of the main obstacles to helping mission clients be productive members of society and not be so lost in this world is getting them to go to work every day and set goals for the future. Most of us who have years of stable employment went to Trade school or college and had dreams for our lives with some kind of job or career in mind that would help us reach our dreams and goals. For most people who are homeless, their only goal is to get through the day; there is no concept of saving money and planning for the future. Many of the people I got to know who came to the mission only wanted to make a few dollars each day to buy snacks, cigarettes, alcohol and/or drugs, and that was good enough. The idea of a long-term job or career was nowhere in their thinking. There is also a sense of entitlement in many of our clients; the world or the government owes them something, and they are waiting on whatever that might be without having to work for it.

In the book, *From Dependency to Dignity,* when people do not have a relationship with God, He sends "shock waves throughout the entire being" (Fikkert and Mask, 90). The authors go on to say that a "severed relationship with God has an effect on human beings that is something like removing a spoke from a tire. The removal of the spoke puts pressure on all the other spokes. They can't hold up under the strain; they start to collapse; and the hub gets damaged as well. Indeed, the entire tire – the whole person – starts to cave in on itself and gets distorted in every dimension. In other words, broken communion with God results in broken relationships with self, others, and the rest of creation. And the damage does not end there, for the Fall also impacts human beings' very substance: minds, hearts, actions, and bodies (Fikkert and Mask, 90). These authors believe that in order to alleviate poverty, rescue missions or any other church or parachurch agency who help, must restore people's communion with God. Any intervention that does not bring the love of Christ to a person in poverty amounts to "trying to repair the hub or strengthen the spoke… without doing the most important thing: replacing the spoke that is missing altogether, i.e. the relationship with the Triune God that can help to make the tire whole again" (Fikkert and Mask, 91). Many people do not understand this concept about the relationship between a desperate and messy life and a relationship with God.

Having grown up in the Church, I have always at least believed in God, and believed that Jesus was the Son of God who came into our world to conquer death, to save and redeem us, and to bring us back into relationship with God since that relationship was broken through sin back in the Garden of Eden as told in the book of Genesis. I admit that as a teen and young adult, I walked away from the Christian faith. Like the prodigal son in Luke chapter 15, I went my own way for a while. However, I never doubted the existence and love of God; I just did not really understand it. I realize many of the men and women who come through the doors of a rescue mission did not have the privilege of growing up in church and were not exposed to the Gospel like I was, but I still wondered - what kept people from believing in God? Why are so many of our clients simply apathetic towards God, as many of the clients I spoke to admitted. Fortunately, I had the opportunity to ask some pressing questions to some of our clients about unbelief and disinterest in God's existence. Guess who showed up again. Remember Damon (from chapter one) who enjoyed living outdoors and who said he did know if there is a God and did not particularly care either? He disappeared for a while but returned again! He still said he did not believe in God, but he wants to, so he came back to the mission where he knew he would at least hear about Jesus…

As a child Damon never attended church services and he had no exposure to the Christian faith. Damon said years ago he was in prison and received a Bible from someone in that prison, "Who came and talked with me once in a while and did the Sunday services." Damon said he started to read the Bible but did not understand it, so he stopped. To get out of his cell, he would attend Sunday service where he listened to this man preach. I told Damon I assumed this preacher was the prison chaplain (or maybe a volunteer), but I have no way of knowing that for certain, and Damon did not know exactly who he was. Damon told me that one Sunday morning while this man was preaching, the police came in, escorted him out of the room, and other inmates heard he was arrested for molesting a child. Damon was crushed and said, "This was the man I looked up to and respected. This was the man I told all of my struggles to and told him very personal stuff about myself. This was supposed to be the 'man of God' and this is what he did? I'm through with that religious stuff. I'm a much better person than this guy! I would never do what they said he did!" Not having ever been in prison, I asked Damon how he knew about this man's arrest and charges, and he said, "Things get around in prison."

I will comment on this particular situation with the assumption that it is true. I have worked as a chaplain for many years. Upon completion of a Master of Divinity from seminary, in order to work as a chaplain, a person has to then complete one year of Clinical Pastoral Education (CPE) at a hospital. I can state firsthand that some of the chaplains I did my CPE with and later worked with were not Christians. One man I worked with was a Muslim. One man was Jewish. One woman was a lesbian Universalist, who did not claim to be Christian, yet read from the Bible. Chaplains do not have to be Christians as many people think; they just need to be so-called "spiritual" people who are of any faith that can endorse and ordain them. So unfortunately if a chaplain commits an egregious sin like child molestation, that person is not necessarily someone who even claims to be a Christian. I am not at all implying that a Muslim, a Jew, or a lesbian Universalist would not also strongly condemn something so grievous as child molestation; I am sure they would, just as a Christian would. What I am saying though, is that the Christian faith is often unfairly targeted, when a person's faith may be unknown, or if that person is of no particular faith at all.

I have also met many people (and I am sure you have too) who claim to be Christians but in reality are not. I know some pastors and chaplains who enjoy the esteem they feel by being labeled "clergy" or the comfortable salaries some clergy receive in large churches or hospitals, yet they do not know the Lord at all. There are several parables in the Bible where Jesus spoke about people who say they know and follow Him, but in reality they do not. One rather frightening instance of such hypocrisy can be found in Matthew 7:21-23: Jesus said, *"Not everyone who calls me, 'Lord, Lord,' will enter the kingdom of heaven, but the one who does the will of my Father who is in heaven. On that day many will say to me, 'Lord, Lord, did we not prophesy in your name, and cast out demons in your name, and do many mighty works in your name?' And then I will declare to them, 'I never knew you; depart from me, you workers of lawlessness.'"* There are indeed people who claim to be Christian and who appear to be "religious" to others, but who are very far from God and perhaps commit egregious sins, like this man at the prison. The "chaplain" who was arrested might not have been of any faith, or he may have been playing the part of a Christian but will be one of those people who hears from God upon his final judgement, *"Depart from me, for I never knew you."*

The Bible does indeed say though, that clergy, teachers, or those with spiritual authority are held to a higher standard of conduct, as they should. James 3:1 says, *"Not many of you should become teachers my brothers, for you know that we who teach will be judged with greater strictness."* A hypocritical "Christian" can be a huge stumbling block for unbelievers. Christians, and especially those who work in full time ministry must walk in a manner worthy of their call (Ephesians 4:1). When Christians openly violate the Word of God, they quickly turn away people who do not believe and stop them from possibly even seeking the truth, like Damon.

I also reminded Damon that if there is a person who calls themself a Christian and commits a terrible sin, that person does not negate the Truth of the Gospel. Christianity is based on the perfect life and love of Jesus – God incarnate - and not on the sins of fallen human beings. We must not discard a perfect Jesus because of imperfect people. The Truth of the Gospel remains, and God is still a perfectly loving God, despite the sins of His people. The Bible condemns the same sins that someone like Damon condemns. The beauty of the Christian faith though, is that the Holy Spirit can change hearts, minds, and lives, forgive the worst of sinners, and make them new creations through Christ. No sinner can take away this beautiful Truth.

Damon also told me that there is simply too much pain and suffering in the world for him to believe in a good God. This dilemma has been around since the beginning of time and has the theological term called *theodicy*. A simple definition of *theodicy* is the vindication of God and attempts to answer the question of why a good God would permit evil in the world. How is an all-knowing (omniscient), all-powerful (omnipotent) and all-good (omnibenevolent) God consistent with the existence of evil and suffering in the world? Unlike a defense which tries to demonstrate that God's existence is logically possible in the light of evil, a theodicy attempts to provide some type of framework where God's existence is even plausible. The German philosopher and mathematician Gottfried Leibniz coined the term "theodicy" in 1710 in his work *Théodicée,* and many philosophers and theologians have wrestled with this conundrum for centuries. There are literally thousands of books written on this topic, and there is no simple answer to this difficult question, other than the free will argument. From the very beginning of time, God gave humanity free will, to choose between right and wrong; unfortunately, people continue to choose the wrong and the evil over the right and the good.

I told Damon that he was in the same company of many great minds who wrestled with the idea of the existence of a good God in such a painful and evil world. I began by explaining the Fall of man as recorded in Genesis chapter three. God originally created the world good, and that there was the first man and woman (Adam and Eve) who lived in a world without pain and suffering, as God meant for them to live in, as well as for all of His creation. However, out of the free will God gave them, they disobeyed His command and sin came into the world, resulting in the pain, suffering, and evil that we have today. Damon looked at me rather strangely and said, "Well I didn't do that! It's not my fault! Why do I have to suffer for their mistake?" I thought that was a good question and I told him that all of us would have disobeyed and done the same thing. God never wanted to force His creation to love and obey Him, but He gave us all free will, which is why we sin. Who wants someone's love through force and without freely choosing to love? God does not, nor would we. God is all good and His desire was for us to live in His Garden of Eden environment forever, in perfect relationship with Him, without pain and suffering.

God gave all of His creation the freedom to make their own choices, including the angels. Lucifer was the most beautiful angel God created, yet he was not satisfied with his position; he wanted to be like God. Stemming from the sins of pride and jealousy, Lucifer did not want to obey or worship God; he wanted to be worshipped. He was thrown out of Heaven, into what we call Hell, along with a third of the angels who were also dissatisfied with their position. Lucifer became Satan and wrecked all of creation, including humankind when he tempted Eve in the Garden. Why is there so much pain and suffering in the world? Because God gave us free will. 1 John 5:19 says that *the whole world lies in the power of the evil one.* God does allow evil, but He is not the creator of evil and He hates evil, much more than we do. Someday God will indeed put an end to evil, but for now, we do of course see evil, pain and suffering in our world. The pain and suffering in this world is not the fault of God – it is our own fault, to the sorrow and displeasure of a perfectly good God.

Another thing I heard from Damon (which I have heard from many people who come to the mission) is that life is so hard here on earth, they do not think Hell can be any worse. Damon asked me, "Don't Christians believe in God so they can go to Heaven after they die? I don't care about what happens after I die; I care about now!" "Well, that is just a part of it" I said. "Many people, like myself, follow God simply because we love Him. Of course we want to go to Heaven after this life is over, but we also want to live meaningful lives here on earth, with purpose, which is what we were created for, and to live life abundantly which is what Jesus offered all of us." Damon laughed and said his life is a living hell now, living alone on the streets in the cold, so surely Hell cannot be any worse. Damon loves nature, so I asked him this question: "Can you imagine waking up in the morning, getting out of your tent, and never feeling the sun on your face? Can you imagine never hearing the birds sing, or seeing a beautiful tree, or smelling a flower? Can you imagine never walking in soft grass or hearing the babbling sounds of a stream? As hard as life might be here on earth for you, at least there is some beauty to enjoy. And what about having no one to care about you? I care about you Damon, as well as other staff at the mission. Yes, life is hard, but there is beauty and love and friendship here that will not exist in Hell. God is still present on earth, but He is nowhere to be found in Hell. Yes, Hell is far worse than the hardest of lives here on earth. Hell has no beauty, no nature, no friendship, and no love, and God does not send anyone there; they send themselves." Damon was silent.

This attitude of not caring about anything more than the present is not only an attitude and mindset of poverty, but also goes back to Maslow's hierarchy of needs that I wrote about in chapter one. If a person's basic physiological needs of food, clothing and shelter are not met (level one) and they are cold and hungry, conversations about God and the afterlife are of very little interest, which is understandable. Damon asked me,

"How does believing in God change the fact that I am cold and hungry? Beliefs aren't important right now." I empathized with him, and said, "Well let's take care of these immediate needs first, which we can help you with here at the mission. We'll talk about God later." An unbeliever has difficulty imagining that God can actually change lives – if we let Him. The issue is, we must allow God to make those changes.

There is also a certain level of fear and anxiety when a person is homeless, so Maslow's second level concerning security and safety need to be met as well before conversations about God are meaningful. Damon told me how difficult it is carrying around everything he owns, and the fear of having his belongings stolen is real, since that happens quite frequently. Living alone on the streets, feeling ashamed when many people either ignore or look down upon a homeless person (which Damon told me he feels) cannot give someone a sense of love and belongingness, which is Maslow's third level. This third level overlaps with level four which is esteem. Damon said when he goes into a store such as Walmart, he feels like other customers are taken care of, but when he needs an employee to help him, he said he is ignored. "Just because I'm homeless doesn't mean I can't pay for what I want and shouldn't be helped like everyone else" he told me.

Damon basically admitted (unaware), that his four levels of needs in Maslow's hierarchy are not met, so a conversation about spiritual matters is of absolutely no interest to him. The beauty of a rescue mission is that they can help meet these first four levels of needs in people, which then allows someone to reach the fifth level of self-actualization where one can contemplate higher thoughts such as the existence and nature of God, and other spiritual and philosophical ideas. Maslow's last level includes pursuing goals; the only goal a homeless person generally has is keeping warm and fed. Christian rescue missions help with basic physiological needs, and after those needs are met, missions can lead people to the love, mercy and grace of the Lord. Damon also told me he did not see how believing in something like God could change his life. Like so many of our mission clients, they have no concept of the broken spoke in the tire that I mentioned above and how not having a relationship with God affects so many areas of life. Perhaps we can replace that missing spoke in Damon's life.

After our conversation, I practically begged Damon to go to walk-ins for some help. I reminded him that the mission can help him secure a job and get housed. He was hesitant, but finally agreed. When Damon was in the office with a case manager, I stopped in to tell him I had to take another client somewhere and had to leave. I sat in the office with him and the case worker for a few minutes, and I could see tears streaming down his face which was hung down as he tried to hide his emotions. I reminded him that both God and I love him. Damon leapt up from his chair, gave me a strong hug, and thanked me. He told me he loved me too. Had it not been for the mission and the many people who care and try to help, Damon would probably be just another statistic and never experience God's love through His people. Damon has a chance to make something of his life, and perhaps to come to know the love of a Savior; that is only possible through Gospel Missions and the people who work and volunteer at them. Like Thomas Merton said, we can find God when we get sick at the sight of ourselves, which describes Damon. He attempted suicide multiple times in the past, but said since he never actually died, he must not be in charge of his death; I agreed. After the mission takes care of Damon's basic needs, perhaps he will then begin to think about God. He now periodically attends chapel services at the mission and Steady Hands and said he is "trying to learn" about the Gospel. Many people, like Damon, would never hear about Jesus in any other place other than a Christian rescue mission. We must also remember that if we are Christ followers, we might be the only representative of the Gospel people like Damon ever see.

Fortunately, there is one man (amongst several) I would like to tell you about who admittedly was very lost in this world. He came to the mission several years ago. His life was a mess and he had no direction or idea what to do about it. Today, thanks to the mission, he is now working full time, has dreams and goals, and is doing very well. He is active in his church and neighborhood as he tries to give back to others because of all that was given to him. His name is Quince.

Quince came to the Mission years ago and went into one of our men's transitional houses (of which I will mention more about in the next chapter). Quince admits that before coming to the Lord, he was very, very lost in this world. Since childhood, Quince suffered immense trauma. His mother was fifteen years old when she gave birth to him, and his father was a 38 year old Vietnam veteran. They never married. Quince said his mother told him that her father beat her and her sisters with tobacco sticks and often raped them.

Quince's father had sex not just with his girlfriend, (Quince's mother), but also with her three sisters, Quince's aunts. One of Quince's aunts became pregnant and had a child by the same man, Quince's father. However, as an infant, this child was suffocated by his grandfather (his mom's dad), so in fear, while still pregnant, Quince's mom left home to go live with her 38 year old boyfriend in fear that her son might be killed as well.

Quince was born, and as he grew older he witnessed his dad beating his mom almost daily, of which Quince thought was normal. One day when Quince was about five years old, he was sitting on his mom's lap and his dad slashed her throat with a knife. Fortunately she was able to get medical help and survived. His mother moved away from Quince's dad after that horrible incident, and they lived with various different people, sometimes living in a car, and then moved into government housing.

Quince describes his dad as a "trained killer" who served in the army during the Vietnam war and who suffered from PTSD. Quince and his mom, along with many other people, feared him. He was also an alcoholic. His dad got a job with the post office as a mail carrier, though he never paid child support and was not very involved in Quince's life. As a child, Quince wondered why he was not "good enough" for his own father to care about him, which left deep scars in his heart and mind.

His mother got a job, and while she worked, she took young Quince to a man who watched him each day, but who also raped him. Quince was about six years old at this time. His babysitter told Quince not to tell his mother about the sexual abuse or he would hurt them both, so in fear, he silently suffered. When his mother finally learned of the abuse, she moved. Quince said he never had any guidance and just ran the streets. His mother later married a man named Ron who worked the third shift and was "mean" to Quince. Ron and Quince's mom had a daughter together, and Quince was often expected to babysit his sister while Ron slept during the day and his mom worked. His mother became involved in drugs, mainly cocaine. She worked as a limousine driver and was supplied with drugs through her job. Quince got into many fights at school, acting out from his anger, and was frequently suspended, which he tried to hide from his mom and stepdad.

Quince often had nightmares about his mother's death which he did not understand but which greatly troubled him. He said his mother was "his whole life" and he really loved her. There were various occasions when Quince said his dad would call his mom and tell her that he was going to pick up Quince and take him to his house for a few days. Quince would gather some things together and wait on the front porch, but his dad never showed up, resulting in more hurt and feelings of rejection and worthlessness.

When Quince was about twelve years old, his dad finally did pick him up and took him to his house for a few days because his mother was in the hospital. He took him to bars that he frequented, and often brought women home and had sex on the couch in front of Quince. Quince noticed that at the bars, many people feared his dad. Quince wanted to be like him. He wanted to be an "army man and a mail carrier" just like his dad, even though he had a poor relationship with him. While staying with his dad, Quince's mom died. He was told that she died of a heart attack in the hospital, but he later found out that she was murdered by someone in the drug business. Quince said his mother had always been paranoid and afraid, and now he understood why.

Quince stayed with his father for a while after his mother's death. His father eventually married, but after a few years, when Quince was in high school, his stepmom left and had an emergency protective order out against Quince's dad since he was violent. Quince also left home and stayed with an aunt until he graduated high school. His aunt (a sister of his late mom) died of a heart attack shortly after Quince graduated high school, so he moved in with some friends and got a job at the mall. He went to community college and graduated with an associate of arts degree.

Quince got into a car accident and was prescribed pain pills, which he did not like. He sometimes sold them and was not interested in drugs because of his mother's death. Many of his friends were involved in drugs though, and eventually Quince began to try various different drugs. He became addicted to morphine and when he tried to quit, he became sick, so he went back to taking this opiate.

A short time later, his father shot and killed himself which really shook Quince's world. All of his childhood trauma, including the death of his mother, seemed to flood over him and he attempted to numb his pain to the point of overdosing. His girlfriend, who he was living with at the time, found him and called the ambulance. He made it to the hospital just in time and was placed on a ventilator; he nearly died. Days later Quince recovered and eventually went back to working at the mall. His girlfriend was a heavy drinker and they eventually broke up.

Quince admitted that he hung out with the "wrong people" and became more involved with drugs. He knew he needed help and a friend told him about a residential program at a church in another state and offered to take him there. Quince agreed. He said it was like a spiritual boot camp with very strict rules and a regimented schedule of prayer, work, and Bible study. Quince got baptized and began his spiritual journey. When Quince finished the program he took a Greyhound bus back home to Kentucky, though he had nowhere to go and was homeless. He moved in with a friend who was very involved with drugs, and shortly after he moved in, the police came with a search warrant and arrested everyone in the house, including Quince.

While Quince was in jail he received an application to the mission's transitional house, the Potter's House, and was accepted when his sentence was completed. Because of the counseling, Bible studies, mentoring, prayer, and the care of the staff at the Potter's House, Quince began to take his faith very seriously and grew strong in the Lord. After many months there, Quince got a job and moved out on his own. Today he is doing well. He works full time at a hospital, goes to three different church services each Sunday and loves the Lord. Quince says it is only the Lord who took him from being so lost in this world to having purpose and joy. He hopes to someday get married and have children and live what he calls a "normal life." Quince attends chapel service at the mission almost every morning, often comes to Steady Hands on Wednesday evenings, and helps anyone in need as he is able. Everyone who knows Quince can see how coming to the mission has drastically changed his life, as well as his eternity since he is a strong Christian man who loves the Lord, as well as the people around him.

I firmly believe that drug use, alcohol abuse, and unemployment are merely symptoms of the main underlying problem of being lost in the world, which is a lack of faith in God and a firm system of belief of who He created us to be. So many people who are lost in this world were never exposed to a loving God or any model of a loving relationship, so they grow up without an understanding of love. Mother Teresa once wrote that when people feel unwanted and unloved, when they are fearful and rejected, they experience a poverty that is very deep and painful with a cure that is much more difficult to find (No Greater Love, 56). When a person finally understands that there is indeed a God in whose image we are all created, who loves us and is deeply involved in our lives, and who has a purpose for each of us, that person is no longer lost in this world. If we truly find God in ourselves when we invite Him into our lives (as Thomas Merton stated at the beginning of this chapter), then a person develops a new self-image and begins to find their way in this world.

Luke 19:10 says, "*The Son of Man came to seek and to save the lost.*" We have all been lost at some point in our lives; some of us are just a little more lost than others.

**Because of her faith and the support of Grace Place,
Ashley said she is a woman of integrity and even when
no one is looking, she wants to do what is right.**

6

Transitional Housing

*"Everyone then who hears these words of mine and does
them will be like a wise man who built his house on the rock.
And the rain fell, and the floods came, and the winds blew
and beat on that house, but it did not fall,
because it had been founded on the rock."*
Jesus - Matthew 7:24 & 25.

"Without faith-based transitional housing, I probably
would not be here today. I have lived in six other transitional
houses, and they never seemed to work; this is the only place
that has really helped me. God has to be in it." Ashley spoke
those words to me as we sat at one of the dining room tables
at Grace Place, the women's transitional house of the Mission.
This lovely old building just outside of the downtown area
of Lexington is really beautiful. Grants and many private
donations made this long-awaited dream for a women's house
possible. Grace Place is a residential program for women
seeking restoration from the effects of addictions, domestic
violence, or homelessness and addresses the complex issues that
have led to destructive life choices, while providing the women
with the tools and support needed to live meaningful lives.

Ashley had been a long-time heroin addict and overdosed
seven times between the ages of 27-35. At age 33 she took
sleeping pills and drank a lot of alcohol in an attempt to kill
herself. Her boyfriend, who she was living with at the time
called 911, which saved her life. What might be some causes
that lead a person like Ashley down such a difficult and painful
road?

Ashley was born in Florida. Her parents split up when she was five years old and she moved with her mom to Louisville, Kentucky where her mother was from and where she still had family. Ashley's grandparents (on her father's side) would drive up from Florida to Kentucky to pick her up each Christmas and summer. Ashley lived with her grandparents during these visits since her father re-married and his new wife did not want Ashley to stay with them. However, her father remained a part and her life and he did spend time with her while she was with his parents.

In the seventh grade, Ashley's mother told her she had to move to Florida full time because she started drinking and smoking marijuana, and her mother could not handle her; she was just too wild. Ashley's mom was an alcoholic, though she did manage to hold a job and had a college education. So Ashley left Kentucky and moved to Florida to live with her grandparents. Life was chaotic for Ashley due to her drinking and drug usage, so she was back and forth from Florida to Kentucky. She was too wild for her grandparents, so she moved back to Kentucky. While Ashley was living in Kentucky, her grandfather died. Her father would not allow her to attend the funeral since she was too much trouble and was involved in drugs at that time. Ashley was very hurt by her dad's decision, but in retrospect she said she understands it and forgives her dad for the hurt that his decision brought her.

When Ashley attempted suicide at age 33, she was taken to a psychiatric hospital. She said she saw hallucinations, probably from her drug use, which really frightened her. She said they were evil hallucinations of her mother being tortured and killed, laying in the bottom of a lake, and other people dying, which frightened her and turned her mind towards God. Ashley believes these hallucinations were of the devil, and she is a firm believer in Satan and evil, of whom she wants to stay far away. These hallucinations were a turning point in Ashley's life which began her journey of faith. In her attempt to quit heroin, Ashley took Suboxone for six years. Today she no longer even takes that, and she is completely clean and drug free. Ashley was arrested about twenty different times for crimes such as theft, writing bad checks, and of course drugs. She spent a total of about two and a half years in jail. All of her crimes were drug-related though, and she believes Satan is very involved in the drug world.

Ashley had a daughter when she was twenty years old with her boyfriend who she said was abusive; they did not stay together. Her daughter lived with her until she was five years old, but then Ashley was arrested and went to jail. Her daughter moved in with her grandmother, Ashley's mother, and is still there today; she is fifteen years old. Ashley said her daughter does not speak to her right now and completely rejects the world of drugs. Fortunately, her daughter is doing well in school, plays on a softball team and has a part time job. Ashley prays for healing in their relationship.

Ashley said her father and his family are Christian and she always went to church with her grandparents when she was with them in Florida. She said her mother and her family were "wild" and did not attend church except for holiday's such as Christmas and Easter. Ashley has been baptized and now attends church regularly, even singing in the choir! She said her father cries happy tears over her now, as does her grandmother, and her mother is very inspired by the change in her daughter's life and is slowing down on her own alcohol consumption. Her grandmother and her mother have visited her where she now lives, at Grace Place, and she firmly believes that there needs to be more faith-based missions and recovery houses in order to change lives. Ashley said Grace Place changed her life and she now knows there is a God who enables her to "keep her integrity." Because of her faith and the support of Grace Place, Ashley said she is a woman of integrity and even when no one is looking, she wants to do what is right.

When I asked Ashley what she now wants out of life, she said she wants to be blessed in order to be a blessing for others. She now has a purpose in life and wants to share the love and healing God gives with others. When we finished our conversation, I prayed for Ashley, and her tears flowed freely. She now has a job, a plan, goals, and a purpose, and most of all, she has hope, which she said she never would have had if it weren't for a faith-based transitional house like Grace Place.

Grace Place was opened after many years of praying and planning for a women's transitional house. Prior to Grace Place, in the early years of the Missions' inception, the Potter's House opened, which is a transitional home for men. Men come here from prison or detention centers, from rehabilitation centers, from homeless shelters, homelessness, or halfway houses, but they all come with unique backgrounds and needs. Usually the men have some form of addiction that makes life unmanageable, such as addictions to drugs, alcohol, gambling, and/or sex.

Potter's House started out as a Christian recovery program but evolved into a transitional living home. This was done at a time when the mission was trying to cut expenses that were not critical to their core mission. Both the Lexington Rescue Mission (LRM) and another ministry in the city were operating recovery programs and neither were filling their beds, so, both ministries agreed to work together to increase the utilization of their services. The other ministry agreed to continue their recovery program, but not start transitional living, and LRM agreed to transition their recovery program into transitional living. By coordinating their efforts, they were able to offer more services to the community, and LRM was able to lower its expenses.

"The Potter's House is a transitional living facility where men realize a growing faith in Jesus Christ, lasting sobriety, and independent living" (LRM Potter's House brochure). The Potter's House has fourteen beds available for men where they teach the residents relapse prevention techniques, life-skills, and monitor support group attendance to help them maintain sobriety. There are many goals the staff hope to achieve who work at the Potters House to help transition their clients back into society, enable them to make good choices, to learn how to deal with their addictions, and to help each man contemplate how he will change his approach to life without these addictions. What will a man's relationship be to God, to others, and even to himself? How will each man personally grow and what goals do they each want to accomplish for themselves? Do they have wives, children, and/or parents who they need to ask forgiveness of and reconcile with? When a man has support from his family, his likelihood of success is much higher.

Some of the basic and practical matters the staff assist the men with are helping them set up payment plans for child support (if needed), make sure they meet their court dates or probation officers when scheduled, obtain identification that was lost (often through incarceration), get a driver's license, and of course, a job.

Many of the men need to learn how to handle finances and also learn how to be good employees. Each man is expected to work, and the staff help them to not only find stable employment, but also teach them how to conduct themselves in a job interview. Clothing is provided as needed so each man will look neat and clean for their job interviews. Also, many of the men need further education or training to obtain stable employment to reach their goals. Unfortunately, there are many men who never even set any goals for themselves or consider their futures, which is also another hurdle to jump.

To achieve some of these goals for the residents of the Potters House, some of the staff teach the *Jobs for Life* class, which helps prepare people to find lasting employment by teaching the skills that will help them succeed in any workplace. This biblically-based class is free and open to the public as well, but it is a requirement for the men at the transitional houses. Other classes that are taught are relapse prevention and conflict resolution. They also deal with issues of pornography and sexual addictions, address problems with boundaries, stress the need for forgiveness, and deal with the guilt and shame that is often present from their past behaviors. Understanding the love and forgiveness of God and feeling the love and acceptance from the staff at the mission makes a huge impact on a person's ability to get past his feelings of guilt and shame, and then learn to see himself as a new creation in Christ. A Christian mission which embraces and teaches God's forgiveness makes these issues of guilt and shame much more impactful and meaningful than a mission that does not teach the Cross and sacrifice of Jesus for the forgiveness of sin. When a person fully understands and embraces the forgiveness of Christ, they can let go of their past and forgive themselves as well.

One component of the Potters House is that the men must be willing to live in a Christ-centered facility and attend several meetings each week such as Alcoholics Anonymous, Narcotics anonymous, Gamblers Anonymous, Celebrate Recovery, and/ or the mission's Steady Hands program. The residents are also expected to attend church on Sunday's and participate in regular Bible studies at the Potters House. They must also be willing to be mentored and discipled by the staff and receive one on one counseling. A humble spirit, an open mind, and a knowledge of a need to change are necessary for transitional housing to be effective. Men must be willing to put forth the effort they need to make changes in their lives, and to be honest and sincere.

Staff try to measure outcomes of success, primarily looking for "Kingdom outcomes" which, of course, are very subjective and individualized. They look for spiritual growth in the men such as the fruits of the Spirit, which are: love, joy, peace, patience, kindness, goodness, meekness, gentleness, and self-control as recorded in Galatians 5:22. Staff assess each man who lives at the Potters House after a certain period of time to see if his speech, his mannerisms, and his thought-processes have changed, as well as his life experiences. Is he now sober? Can he hold a job? Can he learn to live independently and be a productive member of society? These are all crucial issues that are addressed and measured. The outward changes in a man's life reflect the inner changes of the Holy Spirit's work of sanctification. A primary goal of the Potters House staff is to see a man's life change permanently and not have a revolving door of dysfunction. As Christians, the mission staff knows these permanent changes are only possible through the Holy Spirit's work in each of the men who live there.

Presenting the objective Truth of the Gospel is therefore a primary role of Christian transitional housing. More often than not, men who come here have misconceptions of the Gospel and may not believe in a Jesus who came to give us life and give us life abundantly as He promised in John 10:10. When a person grows up in dysfunction and addiction, or falls into that kind of life, the Truth is often hard to find and false beliefs need to be stripped away to allow for the correct Truth of the Christian faith. Some men, thankfully, do change and embrace Jesus as their Lord and Savior, but sadly, some men do not. There is the constant battle of the flesh vs the Spirit, and spiritual warfare is strong in a Christian transitional house, just as it is in the Outreach Center. Trying to maintain a godly, healthy environment at the house is very important, and random drug tests are done frequently, as well as tests done if staff are suspicious of drugs or alcohol. There is zero tolerance for these substances in order to prevent backsliding and an unhealthy environment.

One man I spoke to who is currently living at the Potter's House is Ron. Prior to Ron moving into transitional housing, he was living with his mom, of whom he said he gets along with better when they live separately. Ron's mom is Vietnamese and his dad is American. His parents met when his dad was a soldier during the Vietnam war. Both parents were alcoholic, though both are now sober. Ron's father is now a Christian, but his mother is not and does not profess any particular faith. However, Ron said his mother appears to have some interest in God since he has been at the Potter's House. His parents have been divorced now for about 15 years.

Ron's first brush with the law was when he was only 14 years old. Ron said he was a very troubled youth and has over 100 charges against him with the law, including nine felony convictions. He has spent about 12-15 years off and on in jail. Most of Ron's charges were misdemeanors, but three times his charges sent him to prison. Ron was a drug addict for 25 years, doing any drug he could find, but his drug of choice was heroin. He went to rehab several times, but he said the only thing that really got him sober was Jesus. Ron said even when he was in rehab, he did not really want to get off drugs. He felt very hopeless for so many years and drugs were the way he dealt with his pain. Because of that escape, he had no intention of ever quitting his drug habit, that is until Jesus got a hold of him.

While in jail, the chaplain spoke with him often and Ron attended Sunday services in the jail. He knew about Jesus as a child, but never had the opportunity to grow in his faith. His first introduction to Jesus was through his dad's brother, Ron's uncle. When Ron was about seven years old, his Uncle taught him how to pray and spoke to him about Jesus. Since his parents were not Christian at that time and he did not attend church as a child, he never had the chance to grow in the Christian faith. Teenage years came and he began to get into trouble.

Being in and out of jail so many times, Ron eventually became homeless. He knew Jesus at this time though, and began to minister to other homeless people, trying to give them hope since he knew all too well how life is without any meaning or hope. There is a Lexington Rescue Mission staff member named Chris who would go to the homeless camps, look under bridges and in the woods for homeless people, and tell them about the mission and offer them hope. Ron heard about Chris and wanted to know more about the mission. Through his homeless friends, he found the Outreach Center and came to see if he could volunteer there and if they could help him find a job. Ron had difficulty finding employment because of his criminal record but was told the mission could help him find stable employment despite his record. Ron was offered a job that he found on his own for $15 an hour, but the mission's employment program told him that he could work as a janitor at the Outreach Center to get his foot in the door and prove his work ethic, so he chose the mission work, even though the pay was lower. Ron wants to eventually work in ministry with prostitutes, addicts, and the homeless to offer them hope and show them Jesus, and he feels his janitorial work at the mission is his first step towards reaching his goal. He is very thankful for the opportunity the mission has given him and the trust they have in him to do a good job.

When Ron was initially asked if he wanted to live at the Potter's House, he did not think he needed to since he was now one year sober, he was no longer homeless (he was living with his mom at the time) and was not sure what transitional housing could offer him. He spoke with some of the staff at the Potter's House who told him their number one goal was to help him grow in Christ and that Jesus was the answer to all of life's problems. Ron said that is exactly what he needed since his mother was not very encouraging to him when it came to matters of faith and he was struggling to "move forward." I asked Ron what "moving forward" looked like, and he simply said it meant "growing with God." Ron said he has indeed grown with God since moving into the Potter's House and is very happy there. He said the mission is a great blessing to him where he has access to counseling, structure, Bible studies, and support. He knows the staff cares for him and they help him with basic needs so he can focus on his relationship with God. Ron said since living at the Potter's House he knows he is not alone and is "growing like never before" in his walk with Jesus. He firmly believes that God is using everything in his past, which led him to the Potter's House, to help him in his faith journey and will lead him eventually to his passion – ministering to broken people who need hope through Jesus Christ.

Ron said Jesus found him in his darkest hour when he was alone, homeless, addicted and struggling. He knows that God will use everything that he went through for His glory and that nothing will be wasted. Ron wants to be a witness for Jesus and reflect His love, mercy, and compassion to everyone he comes in contact with. Ron now has meaning and purpose in his life. He appears to have reached Maslow's fifth level because of the support, help, and unconditional love of the mission through the Potter's House. He understands how the Potter's House wants to help him become self-sufficient and they provide all of the tools he needs to reach that goal.

Ron's father picks him up each Sunday and they go to church together. He said they are now very close and have a good relationship. Both his mother and father are grateful for the mission and are happy to see him at the Potter's House where his spiritual and emotional growth are obvious. With each passing day, Ron experiences the deep mercy, grace, love, and forgiveness of God and truly sees how God works all things together for good for those who love Him and are called according to His purpose (Romans 8:28).

The Mission looks at all people as human beings created in the image of God, and love is given to all of the men and women who come through the doors of the mission and the transitional houses. However, rules must also be followed for their own good, just as God gives all of us His rules to follow for our own good as well. The world is full of falsehoods, and it is the job of a Christian mission to show the Truth of the Gospel, which is the only thing that changes lives permanently.

After several years of the Potters House, another men's house was opened called the House of Hope, which is a second step for the men to become self-sufficient and productive members of society. Eighteen beds are available for men in this house. Again, each man is expected to work. Men have more independence at the House of Hope than at the Potters House since they are now in phase two of their transitional living. The men who live here must show growth in their spiritual lives, in their ability to hold a job, and begin the transition of living independently.

When a man successfully completes the program at the Potter's House, he generally moves to the House of Hope. Corey is a man who made this move and is very grateful to the mission that he gets the support and structure from these houses to help him in his new life. Corey was in a faith-based drug rehabilitation facility, and upon completion of the program, he went to live with his dad. While in rehab, Corey did not believe in God. He was not raised with any belief in God and said he only believed in things he could see. He also wondered, like so many people, how could there be a good God when there is so much evil in the world? However, while he was in this rehab facility, he saw other clients get sober, reconcile with their families, and live happy lives. How was this happening to them, but not to him, and how might he change his life in this same positive direction? When he asked other men who lived there with him how their lives were improving, they told him it was God. Several of the men there told him to just "try God" and to pray. He had no idea how to do any of this, but he said o.k. and spoke to a counselor at the House of Hope about how to "try God." He said he believed in God, but in reality, he still did not.

While living with his dad, he still struggled with drugs and felt like he needed to find a sober living house. A staff member of the last rehab place he was in gave him an application for the Potter's House; he had an interview and was accepted. One main issue he had though, were all the rules at the Potter's House that he said he simply was not going to follow. Corey admits that he is rebellious by nature. He did not want to attend any classes, Bible studies, or church services on Sunday and he definitely did not want to be controlled. Corey also said he struggles with anger problems, and after he moved into the Potter's House, he thought, "I want out!" He was taking a shower one day and thinking about packing and leaving, but he said something said to him, "NO! Don't leave. You need the guidance and structure this place offers. Stay." And stay he did. In retrospect, Corey believes that was God speaking to him.

Corey is in his early thirties, and said he struggled with addictions for 21 years. He first tried marijuana when he was only 11 years old, and then tried cocaine when he was just 13. At age 16, he tried opiates, mainly heroin and fentanyl, and was hooked. In and out of jail several times and in prison for four years, he did not have any drug charges but said all of his charges were drug related. He continued to use drugs while in prison and said they are very easy to obtain there. He went to church services in prison to "look good" and to try to feel better and began to believe in God but did not understand much about the Christian faith. His father did not use drugs, though his mother did on occasion and he has several family members who are alcoholics. During his time in and out of jail and in prison, his family relationships were strained, though he said he knows his dad loves him and now trusts him and is a good support to him.

I asked Corey about his life and childhood, and the struggles he may have encountered. When he was 13 years old and his younger brother was 10, his mother left home. Corey bought his mom a Mother's Day gift and had nowhere to hide it, so he stayed at a friend's house the night before so he could surprise his mom the next day. When he came home Sunday (Mother's Day), his father told him and his brother that their mother had left early in the morning and he had no idea where she went. His younger brother was not the natural son of Corey's mother, but she was the only mother he knew. Corey now hated his mother and was upset when he listened to his younger brother cry himself to sleep every night. It was about one month before his mother finally called to tell him that she was living in another state (Indiana - they were in Kentucky). He wrote letters to his mother but was not ready to see her. Eventually, after about a year and a half, Corey and his brother saw their mom. Corey was also angry at the man she was living with for coming down to Kentucky and picking her up, taking her away from her children and home. She eventually married this man, and Corey waited for an apology, but never got one.

Corey was now about 14 years old, and very rebellious. His father was raising the two boys on his own and had very strict rules. He did not want to follow any rules and told his dad, "You can't tell me what to do!" Corey said his dad is "old-school" and believes in authority and rules that should be followed. Since Corey did not want to follow his dad's rules, his father put him on juvenile probation, which meant he had to report to a juvenile officer once a month, but with all of the trouble Corey was getting into at that time, he did not care about the need to report. Soon finding himself in juvenile hall, he still did not want to follow any rules. In retrospect, Corey regrets not listening to his dad who he said is a "good and very smart man" although he does not believe in God.

Corey admits that he struggles with anger problems and was mad at the world. He was angry that his life was the way it was, that his mother left, and that his father acted like he was not hurt when his wife left, which Corey did not understand. His mother signed her parental rights over to his father, which for a young boy was very hurtful.

When Corey was about 28 years old he got married, and he and his wife actually moved in with his mom and her husband. Corey worked with his mom's husband, and they lived there for about 16 months; however. he continued to drink and use drugs. After four years, Corey and his wife separated and they are currently in the process of a divorce.

Corey has two daughters, by two different women: one daughter is fifteen years old, who does not want to see him, and the other daughter is ten, who he occasionally sees, though she lives in Ohio. Corey left the mother of his oldest daughter because of his drug use, so this daughter asks him, "Why do you love drugs more than me?" Corey's eyes were a little teary when he said this to me. However, this older daughter does visit Corey's father, her grandfather, for which he is grateful. Corey wants to see her, but she said she is not ready. Corey thinks of his own mother...

Corey's younger brother, the one who used to cry himself to sleep every night when their mother left home, is currently serving a ten year prison sentence. Corey tells him about his new life and faith in God, and his brother is happy that Corey no longer uses drugs. He tries to help his brother and tells his to pray and to give God a try.

The day I interviewed Corey was Palm Sunday, and he told me he had just been baptized at his church! Corey said he was feeling wonderful and hopes to have drowned his old man in the baptismal pool, and to live a new life in Christ. Corey knows though, that just because he is now a Christian that life is not without pain and struggles, yet in them, he asks God, "What are you trying to teach me?" Corey's fiancé was pregnant with their son, who at eight months died in her womb. Corey said this death shook his faith and his fiancé relapsed and is currently back in drug rehab. Even though Corey does not understand why their little son died, he still believes God is good and asks God, "What are you trying to teach me?" Corey understands, through the help of the staff at House of Hope, that it is not God who takes little babies and brings pain and evil into the world, but it is Satan and the result of the fallen world we live in that brings our sufferings. I reminded him that the way we perceive everything in life is in what we think of God: Is He truly good and does He love us? Does He grieve with us in our pain and suffering? Corey holds onto his faith and tries to encourage his fiancé through this difficult time.

Corey admitted that while living at the House of Hope that he relapsed. He was out with a "friend" who gave him some drugs, and the next thing he remembers is waking up, surrounded by paramedics, who administered Narcan twice and saved his life after taking fentanyl. Corey said his old way of thinking kicked in and he wanted to take control of his life, rather than allow God to take control. Old habits are hard to break. The paramedics wanted to take him to the hospital, but he refused, and instead went back to the House of Hope. A couple of days later, suspicious, the house did a random drug test and Corey's test came up positive for drugs. He had already admitted his relapse and was not sure what would happen to him at this point. The staff at the House of Hope told him he needed to go back to rehab, but Corey was now working full time and did not want to lose his job. He also bought a car and had payments and insurance. His boss told him to go to rehab and that they would hold his job, and the mission paid his car payment and insurance for the month he was away. Corey went to rehab and came back after 30 days.

After being clean and sober for six months, he applied for the house coordinator position that was open at the House of Hope. Generally a person has to be clean for one year, but the staff said Corey had made such great improvements and was no longer the man he used to be, so they hired him. "Only God would have made this possible" he told me. I agreed.

Eventually Corey wants to move out and have an apartment of his own. He admitted that he is not ready yet and wants to grow in his relationship with God and enjoy the support and structure from the House of Hope. He is now learning that he can trust God to see him through his struggles and pains and believes he is alive for a purpose. Corey said he overdosed in the past about six or seven times. One time he was living with a roommate who worked the third shift. For some reason, he came home early one morning and found Corey passed out and his skin blue, overdosed on fentanyl. His roommate called 911 who said in another few minutes, Corey would have been dead; he knows that was God who brought his roommate home early that day. Corey now wants to give back for all that has been given to him by the mission. Corey's life transformation is truly a miracle that may not have occurred without transitional housing and the grace, mercy, and love of God and the staff He uses at those houses.

One of the funniest men I ever met who went through the mission's transitional housing several years ago, is Daryl. He did not come to the mission without huge struggles, but thanks to transitional housing, today he is employed, has an apartment and is doing well. I see him at the mission from time to time, and each time I see him I get a big bear hug and a huge smile. I am simply going to copy verbatim an email I received several years ago from a man named Andrew who ran the Potter's House while Daryl was there since I cannot word it any better:

I was given the honor of taking Daryl to see his daughter who he hadn't seen in three years. He had spent most of her life trapped in his addiction or locked up in prison and had lost custody early in her life. Daryl met with a social worker from Child Protective Services who told him he had done so well in recovery that he was allowed to visit with his daughter again. When he asked how he would get there he immediately mentioned my name (Andrew) since I already told him that I was willing to take him home to see his mother's grave. She died while he was in prison, and he had never seen her burial place.

On the way out of Lexington, I was talking to Daryl about his criminal past. I asked him when the first time was that he had ever been arrested. I was a little shocked at his answer. When he was 12, he was arrested for AI (alcohol intoxication). He said that he started using drugs and alcohol at a very young age. His father died when he was 10, and after that his mother didn't have any rules for the kids to follow. She felt that was the best way to parents her kids.

Daryl's father abused his children. In fact, it was so bad that while his dad was sick and hooked up to an oxygen machine, his dad would beat the kids with his oxygen tubes. When Daryl acted up, his mother would say to her husband that she would beat the kids. She would take them in another room and would hit things and make the kids scream so his dad was satisfied that they were getting what they deserved.

The second time Daryl got arrested was when he was about 13. He told me in the van on the way to his hometown that he beat up the Elvis impersonator at the Chicken Festival. (After Andrew stopped laughing, he asked Daryl to continue with his story). Daryl told me that his mother, who even at 44 years old he lovingly referred to as" mommy" was a huge Elvis fan. There was an Elvis impersonator who was at the Chicken Festival in London, Kentucky who was handing out scarves to people in the audience. Daryl said, "Mommy told me to get her one of those scarves." And so that's what he did. When he got down to where the Elvis impersonator was, he noticed that the scarves

*were only being handed out to pretty young girls. But Daryl
was intent to get what his mommy asked him to get her. And
so he started grabbing for one of those scarves. Finally he had
grabbed one from the Elvis impersonator. The Elvis impersonator
pushed Daryl, apparently out of anger, so Daryl beat up the Elvis
impersonator.*

*When the dust finally settled, the Elvis impersonator yelled
at Daryl, "You can't do that! Who do you think you are?" Daryl
yelled back and said, "Yes I can! I can do anything I want to do!
Who are you?" Then the Elvis impersonator said, "I'm the mayor
of London!"*

If you ever met Daryl, you would not believe this story.
Even though he is a very tall and large man, he is a very sweet
man – a big teddy bear. Daryl continued to struggle, even
while in transitional living, but he came out on the other side
as a man who loves the Lord and people. From his childhood
experiences and turbulent young adult life, Daryl has come a
long, long way and has overcome many obstacles, especially
having a criminal record.

One obstacle to employment is the fact that most of
the people who live in transitional housing have criminal
records which prohibits them from working at many places.
Fortunately, there are quite a few companies who are willing
to give people a second chance and will hire the residents of
the transitional homes. There were some donors to the mission
who asked if some of the residents would cut their lawns, which
grew into a landscaping business of the mission! A man was
hired by the mission to start and run a landscaping business
which is primarily staffed by the men from the Transitional
Houses. This lawn care business is also used as a teaching
mechanism for the residents of Potters House and House
of Hope to become reliable employees, teach them how to

interact with their customers, learn to become self-sustaining, take pride in their work, and learn to support themselves; work is the path to self—sufficiency. This business is also a mutually beneficial way to serve the city of Lexington.   Both the Potters House and the House of Hope are geared towards men who have achieved at least thirty days of sobriety, who have participated in a recovery program and need a safe place to live where they can practice these principles. They are held accountable for their sobriety and actions, and they learn to live sober, healthy, and productive lives. Each man is provided with case management, pastoral counseling, and various life-skills classes.

The average stay for the transitional houses is nine months to a year, though some men stay less, and some stay longer. For men who owe a lot of money in back child support, they may need to stay longer in order to pay their debts, save money for themselves, and become financially independent. For other men who start an educational program in order to get a better job, they too might need to stay longer until they complete that program in order to save enough money to live independently.

Another ministry of the mission that is closely tied to the transitional houses is their ex-offender re-entry program. Specific staff who work with this ministry use a *Breaking Chains* curriculum which provides training and support to assist incarcerated men and women make a smooth transition back into the community upon their release. When the men and women who participate in *Breaking Chains* are released from prison, a case manager meets with them to help them develop a plan to transition back into society and provides accountability and support to help them achieve their goals. Some of these people will come and live in the transitional houses. They also teach the *Jobs For Life* program at the local jails, prisons, and halfway houses.

The men who live at both the Potter's House and the House of Hope, and the women who live at Grace Place all grow in their faith, are given second chances in employment and in life in general, understand personal accountability, and learn to become contributing members of society. They have the opportunity to learn what their God-given gifts are through mentoring and counseling and utilize their gifts in their lives, giving them meaning and purpose which they might not have otherwise ever found. There are truly changed lives from these transitional houses that the Lexington Rescue Mission offers.

"Treat people as if they were what they ought to be and
you help them to become what they are
capable of being."

Johann Von Goethe

7

Changed Lives

"Once upon a time, there was a very wise man who used to go to the ocean to do his writing. He had a habit of rising early to walk on the beach before he began his work. One day as he was walking along the shore, he looked down the beach and saw what looked like a human figure moving like a dancer. He smiled to himself at the thought of someone dancing, no doubt in celebration of the perfect day soon to begin. He was intrigued, so he began to walk faster to catch up. As he got closer, he saw that the figure was a young woman who wasn't dancing at all. Rather she was bending to sift through the debris left by the night's tide, stopping now and then to pick up something, then standing to heave it back into the sea. Curiosity got the best of him so he moved closer and then called out, "Good morning! May I ask what you are doing?" The young woman paused, looked up and replied, "Throwing starfish into the ocean." "Forgive me, but I must ask why are you throwing starfish into the ocean?" said the rather puzzled wise man. "The tide has washed the starfish onto the beach and they can't return to the ocean by themselves. When the sun rises, they'll die, unless I throw them back to the sea."

As the young woman spoke, the wise man surveyed the vast expanse of beach, stretching in both directions beyond his sight. Starfish littered the shore in growing numbers. The hopelessness of the young woman's plan became clear to him and he countered, "But there are more starfish on this beach than you can ever save before the sun is up. Surely you can't expect to make a difference. "At this, the young woman reached down, picked up another starfish and threw it in the ocean. As it met the water, she said, "It made a difference for that one!" Her response surprised the wise man. In fact, he found it quite unsettling. He didn't know how to reply. So instead, he turned away and walked back to his cottage to begin his writings. All day long as he tried to write, the image of that young woman haunted him. He tried to ignore it, but the vision persisted. Finally, late in the afternoon he realized that what the young woman was doing was choosing not to be an observer in the universe, but was, instead, choosing to make a difference. That night the wise man went to bed troubled and when morning came he awoke with a clear vision of what he had to do. So he got up, put on his clothes, went to the beach and found the young woman. And with her, he spent the rest of the morning throwing starfish into the ocean.

"What that young woman's actions represented is something that is special in each and every one of us. We have all been gifted with the ability to make a difference. And if we choose, like that young woman, to put our gift at the service of others we can transform our world. And that is our challenge... to reach down, pick up starfish and throw them wisely and well, and make our world a better place." (Adapted from Loren Eiseley's book, *The Starfish Thrower*).

Many of us are familiar with the above story. I would often remind myself of the *Starfish Thrower* during my time at the mission. The work was often very frustrating and burn-out does exist; it did for me. There were so many people I wanted to see change: become sober, get a job, get off of the streets and be housed, become responsible parents, contribute to society, join a church, and know the Lord. Unfortunately, many of our clients continued in their daily lives without those changes.

Fortunately, there were some people whose lives did indeed change by coming to the mission. I believe that some of the people we came in contact with might change their lives in the future; we planted seeds which, hopefully, they may recall later in life. Since so many people come and go, we never know for sure what becomes of many of our clients. All we can do is pray for them. I cannot tell all of the stories of changed lives that we witnessed at our mission, but I will tell you of a few from people we came to know and love very much.

Developing relationships with our clients was the main thing that kept me working there for six years. Some people could not understand my love for the mission and the clients of whom I got to know pretty well. About seven years prior to working at the rescue mission, I had worked in Calcutta, India at Mother Teresa's Missionaries of Charity, and believe me, working at a rescue mission is much easier that working in Calcutta with the street people of that city. Whenever a rich American visited Calcutta and could not understand Mother Teresa's strong passion for working with the "poorest of the poor," she would say, "We are a contemplative order. First, we meditate on Jesus, and then we go out and look for him in disguise" (Yancey, 233). I agree with Mother Teresa's statement since we should see Jesus not only in our churches and in the great Christian people we know or are at least aware of, but we should also see Jesus in the faces of the broken, suffering people of this world, and understand it is a wonderful opportunity to fulfill Jesus' mandate in Matthew 25:34-40 which says,

> "Come, you who are blessed by my Father, inherit the kingdom prepared for you from the foundation of the world. For I was hungry, and you gave me food, I was thirsty and you gave me drink, I was a stranger and you welcomed me, I was naked and you clothed me, I was sick and you visited me, I was in prison and you

*came to me. Then the righteous will answer him saying,
'Lord, when did we see you hungry and feed you, or
thirsty and give you a drink? And when did we see
you a stranger and welcome you, or naked and clothe
you? And when did we see you sick or in prison and
visit you?' And the King will answer them, 'Truly, I
say to you, as you did it to one of the least of these my
brothers, you did it to me.'"*

Jesus is often disguised in the faces of many of the people
who come through the doors of a rescue mission. Some of
our clients were very, very broken people whose needs were
extensive, but there were others who may not have needed
as much as some of the other clients, but who came to the
mission for other reasons, such as socialization, acceptance, and
unconditional love.

Charlie was a man who I enjoyed visiting with on a daily
basis. He lived about six or seven blocks away from the mission
and walked there every day for lunch and to socialize. What
impressed me about Charlie is that he is blind. He would take
slow, short steps on his walk to the mission using his white cane
and his keen sense of hearing. If a volunteer or staff person saw
Charlie walking down the street on their way to the mission,
they would pick him up. Otherwise, no matter how hot or how
cold it was, Charlie would walk to the mission for lunch. The
only time I can remember him not coming to the mission were
on days when it rained very hard. Charlie did not use drugs or
even drink alcohol, at least not anymore. I am not sure about
his past since we never discussed it. (Charlie was in his 60's
when I met him). He began to slowly lose his eyesight when he
was in his forties, primarily due to macular degeneration and
glaucoma. He never married and had no children.

When Charlie was younger, he worked odd jobs such as
dishwashing, yard work, and maintenance, but as he lost his

eyesight, he stopped working. Charlie had a good sense of humor. He told me that he worked for a day or so as a cook, until his employer realized he could not cook and fired him. I am not sure if that story is true or not since Charlie liked to joke around, but knowing him, it might have happened. Charlie lived with his older sister in a small, modest house, along with many dogs and outside cats that hung around his front porch.

Charlie had no formal education beyond high school, but he was very smart and listened to books on tape of all genres. He seemed most interested, though, in history and politics. He could engage in very interesting conversations, and while he and I strongly disagreed on politics, we respected one another's views and had lively debates. Charlie had never traveled other than the time he spent in the army. He served during the end of the Vietnam War, but he was never deployed to Vietnam. He stayed in Germany for one year and two years in the States and was given an honorable discharge at the end of the war. One place Charlie always wanted to go was Florida to "see" the ocean. In addition to his daily visits at the mission, Charlie stayed active by attending Bluegrass Council of the Blind meetings and outings, and periodic Veteran programs.

When I asked Charlie how he learned about the mission, he said about ten years ago a girl in his neighborhood told him there was a place where he could get a free lunch. She took him to the mission the next day and he started coming every day after that. Charlie is a very interesting man who loves to talk to anyone who takes the time to talk with him. Because he is genuinely interested in other people and asks questions about them and their families, almost everyone likes to talk to Charlie, including me.

During the six years that I worked at the mission, I saw spiritual changes in Charlie. At first, he did not talk about Jesus with me, and it seemed religion was more of an interesting topic of conversation to Charlie than a heart-felt life-changing relationship with God. After talking with Charlie for a couple of years, he said he considered himself a Christian, a Methodist, though he did not attend church. He stayed up late every night listening to the television, so he never got up early enough to attend chapel services at the mission or services on Sundays at a local church. However, Charlie faithfully attended the Wednesday evening Steady Hands program where he listened attentively and sometimes added to the biblical conversations.

Charlie received a government check every month and lived in his sister's house, so he did not utilize many of the services the mission offered such as hygiene supplies, food, housing assistance or clothes. I think one time he took a winter coat when many brand-new coats were donated, and we insisted he take one. His daily visits to the mission were for socialization and a good hot meal. He had food at home, but he could not cook, and I am not sure if his sister cooked; she never came to the mission, though I met her a few times and waved at her as she came to the door or stood on the porch each day when I dropped Charlie off at her house on my way home from work.

There are many needs that are met at a rescue mission other than the material things we think about. People need other people. People need to feel cared for. People long to be heard, to share stories and opinions, and to engage in this world. I often thought of the loneliness so many people feel who come to the mission, especially those who are homeless or even people like Charlie who are not on the streets, but who are single and do not have disposable income for entertainment or travel. In addition to those limitations, Charlie was blind, which I think would isolate him even more.

Rescue missions serve many purposes and have a holistic view of people and their needs, understanding that there are basic physical needs such as food, clothing, and shelter, but there are also social/emotional needs, and of course there are spiritual needs. Missions can surely provide various services to help meet those needs, of which I always appreciated. In speaking of the work Mother Teresa did with the sisters in Calcutta for the street people, she said, "We have drugs for people with diseases like leprosy. But these drugs do not treat the main problem, the disease of being *unwanted*. That's what my sisters hope to provide… The sick and the poor suffer even more from rejection than material want…Loneliness and the feeling of being unwanted is the most terrible poverty" (Yancey, 171). A rescue mission with sensitive workers can help meet that need of loneliness and feelings of not being wanted or accepted in society. I asked Charlie once if he felt lonely and he told me no. He said the people at the mission were his "friends" and he enjoyed their company; the mission accomplished that need.

There was a large blackboard in the lunchroom that I would write on each Monday. Sometimes I would write an important announcement such as a change of time for some particular service or information on an upcoming event. Most weeks though, I would write a biblical or philosophical question for the clients to ponder in hopes of starting some meaningful conversations. I would read the question before I said the prayer for lunch each day, and I was pleasantly surprised with some of the answers or comments some of the clients had in response to my questions. Charlie would always ask me, "What's the question of the week?" and he would always have some type of answer – usually a thoughtful one. Some weeks I would simply write a verse out of the Bible and ask the clients what it meant. I was perhaps overly optimistic about starting spiritual conversations, or at least thoughts concerning God and the Christian faith, but as the chaplain I persisted week after week, year after year. To my delight, I would occasionally hear people talk about the question at the lunch tables, or sometimes a client would stop me in the hallway to engage in conversation surrounding my questions.

When I would be away on vacation, Charlie would often have a volunteer or staff person leave a note on my desk for when I came back, suggesting a question or a thought for the week upon my return. Near the end of my time at the mission, Charlie's notes became more spiritual in nature. One note read, "As you climb the mountain you called on Me. As you crossed the valley, I carried your soul." Another note he left for my return said, "I will trust in the Lord in my days and nights, singing Your praise. I will climb my mountains, spreading Your seeds. I will cross all rivers and streams, praising Your name. In Jesus name, amen." I was very happy to know Charlie began to think more and more about spiritual matters and wanted me to know of his thoughts. Everywhere he went, he would tell people, "God bless you." The mission not only fed Charlie lunch and provided socialization for him, but it also strengthened his relationship with God and showed him the love of Jesus Christ of which he shared with others.

Tye was another regular client who has a very interesting story that he wants to share with everyone he meets, and he pretty much does that! I will tell his amazing story shortly, but first a bit about him. Tye is a large imposing looking man, about 6'5" and well over 250 pounds, but from what I knew of him, he seemed like a gentle giant. For much of his teen and adult life, Tye was involved in drugs. He grew up in Tennessee in government housing and quickly discovered that selling drugs was an easy way out of poverty. As a young man, having nice clothes and a flashy car was enticing, which also attracted the ladies. Tye and his first wife had two daughters, but unfortunately his wife died fairly young of cancer. Tye now has several grandchildren of whom he is very proud. He loves his daughters and their children and spoke of them often to me. I would hear him talking to them on the phone almost every day when he was at the mission. He loves his family.

Years later Tye re-married, and both his new wife and he became very involved with drugs. Tye did not talk much about his past, only small glimpses that I tried to piece together. He was much more concerned with his present life as a Christian and said he did not want to go back to that "old man." I agreed. For the years that I knew Tye, he read his Bible, attended church most Sunday's, came to the chapel services at the mission frequently, and was a regular for quite some time at our Wednesday evening Steady Hands program. Tye would come to my office to talk almost every day and we got to know one another quite well. Sometimes he would just tell me about his days, his thoughts, and his growing faith, and sometimes he would seek counsel and ask me various questions about his direction in life. Some days he just wanted me to pray for him. After about a year or so of long conversations, Tye told me he wanted to get baptized and asked if I would baptize him; I was more than happy to do that! I arranged for him to be baptized at the church of the other Pastoral Care Coordinator and requested help from one of the elders since Tye was such a large man and I did not want to drop him in the baptismal pool. We agreed on a day that following week and invited a few people to attend and we all rejoiced at this special event. Tye did well for about a year. He regularly attended chapel service and Steady Hands and continued to come to my office to talk and pray.

Unfortunately, his wife was often in and out of jail, but he really loved her. Tye said he looks out of his kitchen window every day, waiting for her to come back home and he greatly missed her. Tye was very committed to relationships, and family was very important to him. He spoke to me about his mom quite a bit as well. Tye had a descent apartment down the street from the mission, but said he wanted to move to another side of town where there were less drugs and begin his life with his wife again when she came home from jail, which would be soon. He moved into a second floor apartment of a house about a mile away, on the other side of the tracks, and got everything ready for her arrival. Tye came to the mission to tell me she would be home the following day, that he would bring her over for me to meet her and was excited about this next chapter in his life. However, that next day, he disappeared. I did not see him for several months and worried about the direction of his life.

Eventually Tye returned to the mission and looked rough. He was now homeless. When I asked what happened to the apartment he got for he and his wife, he said he could not pay the rent and was back on the streets. I asked him directly if he could not pay his rent because he was using drugs again, and he admitted that was indeed the case. It seemed that whenever his wife came back into his life after being in jail, he would fall back into his "old man" and started using drugs again. It broke my heart to see Tye in this condition. It was cold out and he asked me to save any cardboard we had from boxes of items that came to the mission. I asked what he wanted the cardboard boxes for, and he said he used them to light fires at night to stay warm. I continued to ask Tye to get some help and wanted to get him off the streets. He broke my heart every day that I saw him, especially since he was now such a different man from the one I originally met. When Tye first came to the mission, he looked healthy, he always spoke about Jesus and his faith, about his church and his pastor, and about how God works in his life, always "in three's" he would say. He was excited about being a Christ-follower and spoke to everyone about Jesus. Now, he seemed empty, alone, and lost, even though I knew he still loved the Lord. The drugs simply had a hold of him and he would not let them go.

After several months of talking and praying with him again, almost daily, I called Scott and we got Tye into rehab and off the streets. He was finally ready. I did not see him for a few months, but eventually he was given more freedom and was able to visit the mission again as he advanced through the program. Usually the people who go to rehab are expected to find a job and work full time. Tye however, could not work due to a gunshot wound from years ago, and here is the amazing testimony he loves to tell everyone he meets:

Tye and his second wife were living in Memphis, Tennessee. They were heavily involved with drugs, including the selling of them. He was walking near the apartment complex where they lived, when suddenly a man came around the corner and shot him in the head, "execution style." He knew he had been shot, and was able to say, "Man, you shot me" as he fell to the ground on his knees, then onto his face and passed out. Someone saw him lying in a pool of blood and called 911 and he was quickly taken to a hospital. After his immediate wounds were addressed, Tye was transported to a nursing home where he remained in a coma for about 30 days. One day when his nurse was caring for him, she suddenly shouted, "This baby woke up!" To everyone's surprise, Tye slowly came out of his coma. Then she said, "Boy, I have a son your age!" and the third thing she said was, "You're gonna get out of this bed and walk!"

Tye said he will never forget those words and was determined to walk again, which of course in time, he did.

Tye had no recollection of being in a hospital for about a month prior to going to the nursing home/rehabilitation center since he was in a coma. It was a miracle that he survived. He had to learn to talk and walk again and was in rehab for quite a while. Even though Tye had been involved with drugs at the time of his shooting, he still knew the Lord and credited God for saving his life. Sometimes, like so many people who came through the mission, they love the Lord but cannot get that monkey (drugs) off their back. Tye worked hard in his rehabilitation and learned to walk, talk, and function normally again. Other than the area on his head that has a slight dent and scar, no one would know that Tye had almost been killed. His recovery is truly a miracle, and he gives all the credit to God whenever he tells this amazing story.

In retrospect, Tye said he believes God talks to him in three's, starting from his nurses' three statements at his bedside at the nursing home. He also said his recovery went in three stages: (1) he went from his bed to (2) a Gerry chair, then (3) to a walker. When he finally decided to seek treatment years later for his drug problems, his room at the rehab center was number three; Tye said he believed that was the place God wanted him to be and would help him with his addictions. His daughter went to college to become a third grade teacher. He comes from a family of three boys. After being homeless for a while, he moved to Third Street and there was the number three in his address. Throughout the Bible God spoke to people through many different ways, and He has not ceased. God knows each of us individually and intimately, and Tye believes that he discerns the voice of God when he sees patterns of three's.

When I asked Tye what the most important thing in his life is, especially surrounding the shooting and his near death, he said, "Never give up on God." He said he knows what it's like to be at "rock bottom" and that when a person is there, he admitted, they are "losers." Tye said he wants to be a winner and stay with the Lord and follow His will for his life.

The mission gave Tye hope, acceptance, and love, and never judged him, even when he fell and began using drugs again. When Tye backslid and fell back into drugs, the mission got him into rehab and gave him another chance. The staff at the mission never gives up on God, and because of that faith, they never give up on people either; Tye knew that and said he loves the mission. He is still clean and sober and living in transitional housing, telling his testimony to everyone who will take the time to listen to him. He comes to the mission as often as possible, attends chapel services, Steady Hands, and continues growing in his faith.

For years, two brothers, Len and Don came to the mission every day, and the staff and volunteers got to know them well. They had been living down the street from the mission with several people and heard they could get a free lunch there, so they came. Both men were in their late 50's and looked worn. They were both heavy drug users for many years. Don had a wife (or an ex-wife, it was not really clear) who was in Florida who he spoke to on occasion, but no children. He had worked as a carnie for years but was currently not employed. Len never married and had no children. He had worked maintenance for many years, but like his brother, he was no longer working either. They were poor and hungry, so they came through the doors of our mission.

Thomas, the other Pastoral Care Coordinator got to know them very well and spent a great deal of time with them. He invited them to chapel, strongly urging them to attend, and they did. They both grew to love Thomas and became regular "fixtures" at the mission. They came to Steady Hands every week, and Don became a volunteer at the mission. He helped in the kitchen and he served soft drinks at Steady Hands. He also helped our maintenance man and did whatever he was able to do each day; he found new purpose in his life through the mission. Thomas helped Don and Len get some clothes, and Don even began wearing suits and ties every day to the mission which he got from someone who donated them. Len dressed much more casually, but he looked much better and cleaner than when he first came to the mission. Both men eventually gave their lives to the Lord and were baptized at Thomas' church. They were happy and wanted to give back to the mission for all they received, which is why they came every day and helped out wherever they could. Their gratitude was obvious.

Our staff worked hard to get them an apartment. They wanted to leave the house they were living in since it was basically a drug house and they were trying to turn their lives around and leave the world of drugs. Most of their lives though, they had both been involved with drugs so this new life was a huge change for them, and also a huge challenge. They were both determined though, and everyone seemed to get involved in the lives of these two brothers who had made such a dramatic change in their lives; after all, that is why the mission exists.

It was not very long when our housing coordinator found them an apartment. It took two buses to get from this apartment to the mission, but they were ready to make the move. Volunteers donated sheets and towels, kitchen supplies such as dishes and pots and pans, a table and chairs, a couch, two beds, and we were able to move them in to a well furnished apartment. They were thrilled, and so were we! Most days, the other Pastoral Care Coordinator, Thomas, would pick them up and bring them to the mission. When he could not, they would take the two buses necessary to get to the mission. It seemed like these two men had really changed their lives.

Slowly over time, they stopped coming every day. When Thomas would go to pick them up, they were high. After almost two years of coming to the mission, these two brothers appeared to have fallen back into their old way of life. They stopped paying their rent since their money went to drugs instead, and they were evicted from the apartment that we all worked so hard for them to have and to furnish. The staff and the volunteers who loved them and had been involved with their lives were very disappointed.

Don and Len moved in with some family members, but they all used drugs as well. Don stayed with his family, but Len said he was ready to finally give up the drugs for good but admitted he could not when he was around it all of the time, so he left. Leaving his family who he loved was difficult, but Len loved the Lord more and wanted to live a productive Christian life which he knew he could not do while living with his family. The housing coordinator at the mission put Len on a list for a government subsidized apartment because of his modest income, but nothing was available yet, so Len moved into the men's homeless shelter down the street; he was determined to return to his changed life as a sober Christian man.

Shortly after Len became homeless and moved into the shelter, we spoke to Lee who was running the men's transitional houses for the mission and asked if they would take Len. He took him that day. Len stayed at the Potter's House for quite a while and grew in his faith and commitment to a new life.

After many months there, with a lot of mentoring, Lee thought he was ready for his own apartment again and the housing coordinator found him a place of his own. Len admitted that he was tempted to use drugs from time to time, and said he did not live without any struggles, but he felt the unconditional love and encouragement from the people at the mission and he thanks God that he and his brother walked down to eat lunch years ago. The mission saved his life. As for his brother Don, he remains back in the world of drugs, but we pray that like his brother, he will get tired of that life and return to the new life he found in Christ through the mission. For Len, that one starfish, his life was saved. We planted the seeds in Don, as we do in so many people who walk through the doors of the mission - and wait.

Unfortunately, a few years after Len moved into his own apartment, he was diagnosed with stage four cancer and given six months to two years to live, depending on how much treatment he was able to withstand. What if Len had never come to the Mission? What if no one ever reached out in love to him, shared the Gospel of Jesus Christ with him, took him to get baptized, and simply came along side of him and loved him? When I visited Len and asked him about his diagnosis and his faith, he said he was not ready to die, but he knew he would be with the Lord and expressed his gratitude to the mission and all of the people he met there. Remember that starfish story? Len was one of many who found hope, found love, and found the Lord through a Christian gospel mission. God often works with and through one person at a time to show His love, save His people, and bring them home to Him. What a wonderful opportunity to be a part of a place where God works so powerfully.

8

Who is Jesus Anyway?

"Now it happened that as he (Jesus) was praying alone, the disciples were with him. And he asked them, 'Who do the crowds say that I am?' And they answered, 'John the Baptist. But others say Elijah, and others that one of the prophets of old has risen.' Then he said to them, 'But who do you say that I am?' And Peter answered, 'The Christ of God'"
Luke 9:18-20

One particular man who frequented the Mission from time to time wrote on his prayer card during walk-ins one day, "That it will be revealed to me whether God does or does not intervene in human life, be it fortune or misfortune." I found his question quite interesting. There is indeed a spiritual hunger in people that a rescue mission can help fill, and the clients who asked me about the existence and nature of God made my job as a chaplain quite exciting. Of course as a Christian, I believe God does indeed intervene in human life out of His great love for us. A different point of view comes from people who call themselves "deists," who believe that God created the world and then walked away from it with disinterest. Working at a rescue mission allowed me to see a very compassionate and loving God at work, intervening in many people's lives in order to point them to Him and to His love. On a daily basis at the mission I saw a loving God very interested in His creation and in the lives of His people and had the wonderful privilege of seeing God change hearts, minds, and lives of many people who came through our doors. Working at a rescue mission allowed me to see God in a different light than I formerly had seen Him.

Many of us who have grown up in middle-class families and who attended worship services every Sunday may not fully understand who Jesus is from the Sunday school lessons and sermons we have heard all of our lives. We may have grown up thinking that going to church each Sunday and being good, moral people made us good Christians. Some people think they are going to Heaven because they never committed the "bad" sins, as perhaps some of our clients have committed. A careful reading of the Bible shows us a different Jesus than some of us have learned about in church or who we imagine Him to be. Jesus never shied away from the prostitutes and sinners, so neither can we. Working at a rescue mission around people who are very different from myself helped show me a Jesus I had not really understood in the past; one who is far more merciful and compassionate to people who are far from Him, and whose love knows no bounds. I saw the hand of a powerful God during the daily work that takes place at a mission, and I now have a deeper understanding of His heart for the poor and the lost.

Before I got to know many street people, I did not look upon them as possibly my brothers and sisters in Christ. However, after many conversations with so many homeless people, I realized that some were indeed followers of Jesus, but could not get over their troubled pasts and continued to deal with addictions as they struggled with their private demons. How many dirty, worn-out people standing on a street corner holding a cardboard sign have we all passed by and never gave them a second thought? Perhaps in our self-righteousness we may have felt some compassion or pity for them, but we failed to see them as human beings created in the image of God and for whom Jesus died and wants in His Kingdom.

In his book *The Jesus I Never Knew,* Phillip Yancey wrote, "In his own social interactions, Jesus was putting into practice 'the great reversal' heralded in the Beatitudes. Normally in this world we look up to the rich, the beautiful, and the successful. Grace, however, introduces a world of new logic. Because God loves the poor, the suffering, the persecuted, so should we. Because God sees no undesirables, neither should we. By his own example, Jesus challenged us to look at the world through what Irenaeus would call 'grace-healed eyes'" (Yancey, 155). Phillip Yancey goes on to say, "If we cannot detect God's presence in the world, it may be that we have been looking in the wrong places" (Yancey, 232). Where are we looking for God? Do we ever see Him in the faces of the homeless or the struggling addicts? Mother Teresa often said she saw Jesus in the faces of the poorest of the poor. Sometimes we fail to see Jesus because we do not know what He looks like or how and where He reveals Himself.

God reveals His character throughout the Bible and allows us to get a glimpse of what He is like. As a Christian, I believe in the incarnation; God came to earth as a man, Jesus Christ and lived a perfect life. When we read the New Testament, especially the four gospels, we read about the interactions Jesus had with many different types of people. Jesus saw all people in need of His love and redemption, and He appeared to have sought out the undesirables, the outcasts, and the unclean to teach the religious people of His day, as well as His disciples, how we are to view and treat every kind of person. There is a saying that all people are equal at the foot of the Cross. We all sin. We all need forgiveness. We all need to change and become more like Jesus. In order to become more like Him though, we need to understand His character.

There is a difficult passage about Jesus in the gospels of Mark chapter 7 and Matthew chapter 15, where Jesus spoke to a Gentile woman, and seemingly calls her a dog! The gospel of

Mark calls the woman a "*syrophonecian*" but Matthew labels her as a "*Canaanite.*" Mark identified this woman's nationality, which describes a native or inhabitant of Phoenicia when it was part of the Roman province of Syria, in other words, a Gentile, when he used the word *syrophonecian.* The term Matthew used though for Gentile, was "*Canaanite,*" which had not been used for centuries. Using the term *Canaanite* to describe the woman Jesus spoke to in these chapters would be the equivalent of us calling someone from Britain an *Anglo Saxon* or a *Celt,* labels we do not use anymore. Matthew had a theological reason for using this outdated term. The Canaanites were the people who lived in the Promised Land prior to the invasion and arrival of the Israelites under Joshua in the Old Testament. The Canaanites were a polytheistic people who worshipped many gods, including El and Asherah, which included child sacrifice and temple prostitution. While Mark basically wanted us to know that Jesus spoke to a Gentile woman, Matthew wanted to convey that this woman was a complete outsider, an enemy of the Jewish people, perhaps not even worthy of God's grace. Let's look at the passage in Matthew 15:21-28:

"*And Jesus went away from there and withdrew to the district of Tyre and Sidon. And behold, a Canaanite woman from that region came out and was crying, 'Have mercy on me, O Lord, Son of David; my daughter is severely oppressed by a demon.' But he did not answer her a word. And his disciples came and begged him saying, 'Send her away, for she is crying out after us.' He answered, 'I was sent only to the lost sheep of Israel.' But she came and knelt before him, saying, 'Lord, help me.' And he answered, 'It is not right to take the children's bread and throw it to the dogs.' She said, 'Yes, Lord, but even the dogs eat the crumbs that fall from their masters' table.' Then Jesus answered her, 'O woman, great is your faith! Be it done to you as you desire.' And her daughter was healed instantly.*"

Jesus' disciples did not want to give this woman the time of day since she was not Jewish, and perhaps she might have even been a prostitute. Scripture does not say anything about this woman's character – just her nationality. However, the term "dog" was applied to cult prostitutes in the ancient Near East in the Canaanite worship of Asherah, to *"reflect their faithfulness to the profession"* (Archeology Study Bible, footnote, 267). Biblical scholars generally agree that the Canaanite worship of Asherah was gone by the time of Jesus, so I am not implying that this woman was a temple prostitute, but there is a possibility that Jesus might have been conveying something about her character. We note that at first, Jesus did not speak to her. What or who was He waiting on? The disciples were with Him, and they were quick to speak and told Jesus to leave her alone. Jesus ignored them. What was He trying to teach them? Perhaps that He loves all people, even His enemies or any outsider or sinner. Everyone is invited to be in relationship with Him and can find forgiveness when they seek it. Remember, as Jesus was literally being crucified, He said, *"Father forgive them, for they know not what they do"* (Luke 23:34). No one is too far from His love and mercy.

The Jews in Jesus' day sometimes referred to all Gentiles as "dogs." In Greek, the word for dog is *kuon,* which means, "wild cur" and is used in Matthew 7:6, Luke 16:21, and Philippians 3:2. Non-Jews, or Syrophoenicians, were considered by Jews to be so unspiritual that even their presence could make a person ceremonial unclean (John 18:28). So why would Jesus even go with His disciples to a Gentile "neighborhood" where He encountered this Canaanite woman? Jesus Himself said His mission was to the "lost sheep of Israel," in other words, the Jewish people, not the Gentiles or as Matthew wrote, the "Canaanites." Ministering to this Canaanite woman would take His time away from the Jewish people. The Greek word Jesus used though in this conversation when He implied that this woman was a dog was *kunarion*, which means "small dog" or "pet dog," which is obviously a different word from *kuon*, which was used for unspiritual people or unclean animals. However, could Jesus have been referring to the ancient Canaanite religion with the particular word He chose?

So what was Jesus doing in this passage? How did He perceive this Canaanite woman? Jesus often tested people through conversations and questions. There is the story about the woman at the well in John chapter 4. Jesus passed through another Gentile town, Samaria, which was a town where people lived who the Jews did not like. Samaritans were half Jewish and half Mesopotamian colonists. The Mesopotamians were also people who worshipped other gods. In this passage in John, it says,

"A woman from Samaria came to draw water. Jesus said to her, 'Give me a drink.' (For his disciples had gone away into the city to buy food). The Samaritan woman said to him, 'How is it that you, a Jew, ask for a drink from me, a woman of Samaria?' (For Jews have no dealings with Samaritans). Jesus answered her, 'If you knew the gift of God, and who it is that is saying to you, 'Give me a drink,' you would have asked him and he would have given you living water...' Jesus said to her, 'Go call your husband, and come here.' The woman answered him, 'I have no husband.' Jesus said to her, 'You are right in saying 'I have no husband;' for you have had five husbands, and the one you now have is not your husband.' (John 4:7-10 & 16-18).

Once again we see Jesus talking to a non-Jewish woman of questionable character. Both sections of Scripture, the Canaanite woman, and the Samaritan woman, are two instances of Jesus breaking cultural norms. Men in the Jewish culture of Jesus' time were not supposed to speak to women in public who were not members of one's family, and Jewish people were not supposed to speak to Gentiles, yet Jesus took His time to hear what both women had to say and to minister to their needs. Jesus recognized the faith of the Canaanite woman from the first section of Scripture and healed her daughter (Matthew 15:28). With the Samaritan woman at the well, Jesus took the time to reveal who He was and to share with her the opportunity for salvation, as well as the entire town, since the passage goes on to say, *"Many Samaritans from that town believed him because of the woman's testimony."* Jesus even stayed in the Samaritan town for two more days at their request (John 4:40). Jesus was certainly not following the cultural and religious norms of the day!

Most of us know the parable of the Good Samaritan found in Luke 10:25-37 where Jesus broke several cultural and religious norms of His day. A lawyer questioned Jesus about how to obtain eternal life, and Jesus quoted the *Shema* as found in Deuteronomy 6:5 which says, *"You shall love the Lord your God with all your heart and with all your soul and with all your might"* and then He quoted Leviticus 19:18 which says, *"You shall love your neighbor as yourself."* When the lawyer asked who his neighbor was, Jesus told the parable:

A man was going down from Jerusalem to Jericho, and fell among robbers, who stripped him and beat him and departed, leaving him half dead. Now by chance a priest was going down that road, and when he saw him he passed by on the other side. So likewise a Levite, when he came to the place and saw him, passed by on the other side. But a Samaritan, as he journeyed, came to where he was, and when he saw him, he had compassion. He went to him and bound up his wounds, pouring oil and wine. Then he set him on his own animal and brought him to an inn and took care of him. And the next day he took out two denarii and gave them to the innkeeper, saying, 'Take care of him, and whatever more you spend, I will repay you when I come back.' Which of these three, do you think, proved to be a neighbor to the man who fell among the robbers? He said, 'The one who showed him mercy.' And Jesus said to him, 'You go, and do likewise.'"

There are several culturally and even religiously inappropriate situations in this parable. First of all, Jesus mentioned that the hated Samaritan was the only person who acted correctly in this story. Jesus also used a priest and a Levite as the two men who ignored the hurt man; why? This man who was beaten and surely bleeding would have been considered unclean by Jewish law, which is why these two men crossed over to the other side of the road so they would not even come near him and become unclean themselves. But the Samaritan, the Gentile, obviously did not follow the Jewish laws of what was clean and unclean, and simply chose to help this man. Jesus once again showed that there is no such thing as a clean or unclean person, but that we are all equal in God's sight and all people are worthy of love. Also, the Samaritan left the man at the inn and said he would be back, so it is obvious that he had some place he needed to be, yet he took his time to help. Jesus also took His time to speak with the women of whom He wanted to help who were considered unclean either by their ethnicity or their sins.

We have another story in the gospels about Jesus' interaction with yet another woman of questionable character who was caught in the act of adultery. John 8:1-11 tells the story of a woman who was brought to Jesus by the scribes and Pharisees (the religious leaders of that day) who asked Jesus if she should be stoned, according to the Law of Moses (John 8:5). At first, Jesus said nothing, but simply *"bent down and wrote with his finger on the ground"* (John 8:6). Again, Jesus remained silent (like He did with the Canaanite woman), perhaps wanting to teach the religious leaders around Him something. He paused. We have no idea what Jesus wrote on the ground, but He then said, "*Let him who is without sin among you be the first to throw a stone at her*" (John 8:7) and bent down and wrote on the ground again. After the scribes and Pharisees walked away, "*Jesus stood up and said to her, 'Woman, where are they? Has no one condemned you?' She said, 'No one Lord.' And Jesus said, 'Neither do I condemn you; go, and from now on sin no more'*" (John 8:11). Yes, Jesus' grace, mercy, and forgiveness is far deeper than we may sometimes understand.

There are other instances of Jesus doing culturally and religiously inappropriate things. For example, when Jesus healed someone, He often touched them, even though they were considered unclean. He could have just spoken a word from a distance like He did in Luke 7:1-10 which tells the story of a centurion who had a servant who was very sick and near death. When the centurion heard that Jesus was in his town (Capernaum), he sent some elders of the Jews to ask Jesus to come and heal his servant. The elders pleaded with Jesus on the centurion's behalf, so Jesus went with them. As Jesus came near the house, the centurion sent some of his friends to tell Jesus that he did not feel worthy to have Jesus in his home but asked if Jesus would just "*Say the word, and let my servant be healed. For I too am a man set under authority, with soldiers under me: and I say to one, 'Go' and he goes; and to another, 'Come,' and he comes; and to my servant, 'Do this,' and he does it*" (Luke 7:7-8). When Jesus heard what this man said and marveled at his faith, He healed his servant right where He was, without entering the centurion's house. Verse 10 of this section of Scripture says, "*And when those who had been sent returned to the house, they found the servant well.*" Jesus did not need to even be near a person to heal them, yet He made it a point to frequently touch those He healed.

There are at least fourteen instances where Jesus touched the person He healed and at least four instances where people touched Him in order to be healed. There was a man Jesus touched with leprosy in the city of Galilee found in Matthew 8:2-3, Mark 1:40-42, and Luke 5:12-13. Then we read of Jesus healing Peter's mother in law by touching her in Capernaum in Matthew 8:14-15 and Mark 1:30-31. Jesus laid His hands on many sick people in Luke 4:40, and healed a 12 year old girl in Matthew 9:25, Mark 5:41-42, and Luke 8:54-55. He also healed two blind men in Capernaum in Matthew 9:29-30 by touching them, and a few people in Nazareth in Mark 6:4-6. Mark 7:32-35 records Jesus touching a deaf man to heal him in Decapolis, and a blind man just outside of Bethsaida in Mark 8:22-25. A blind man in Jerusalem was healed in John 9:1 by Jesus' touch, and in a synagogue, a woman who could not stand straight was healed by Jesus' touch in Luke 13:11-13. Two blind men were healed near Jericho in Matthew 20:30 and the servant of the high priest whose ear Peter had cut off was healed with the hand of Jesus in Luke 22:50-51. There are also two cases where Jesus' touch occurred very close to the time of healing in Luke 7:14-15 where Jesus raised the young son of a widow, and the healing of a young boy in Mark 9:25-27. People who touched Jesus to receive a healing are recorded in Mark 3:10, Luke 6:18-19, and Matthew 9:20-22, and Matthew 14:35-36.

The Old Testament frequently mentions anyone who touched an "unclean" person (a person with any illness or disease) was then also considered unclean. However as we just saw, the Bible records many instances where Jesus touched people to heal them when He certainly could have just spoken a word and kept His distance. It seems to me that Jesus knew the power of human touch and used it even when He did not need to. After all, He was God, and God created everything simply by His Word. Perhaps Jesus' touching "unclean" people was one more way to show that no one is really unclean. Remember Peter's vision? In Acts 10:9-16, Peter was hungry and went up on a housetop to pray. He fell into a trance and saw the heavens open and what appeared to be a large sheet descend before him which held all kinds of unclean animals. A voice told Peter to eat, but Peter said, *"By no means, Lord; for I have never eaten anything that is common or unclean. And the voice came to him again the second time, 'What God has made clean, do not call common.' This happened three times, and the thing was taken up at once to heaven"* (Acts 10:14-16). The Jewish people separated themselves from the non-Jewish people (Gentiles) and were not allowed to eat with them since the Gentiles ate "unclean" food. Peter's vision taught him that nothing and no one is considered unclean to God, even those who were sick or sinful.

There is something about the power of touch which I found to be an important component in my work at the mission. Just a touch on someone's shoulder or arm might have been more human physical contact than many people who came through the mission had received in a long time. Sometimes a very dirty homeless person would be happy to see me and spread their arms wide to hug me. I will admit, I was sometimes a bit leery to hug them, but I made it a point to receive and to give a hug. There is indeed power and the feeling of acceptance in a simple hug.

We can also look at the ordinary people Jesus entrusted Himself to and used to spread the Gospel and start His Church. John Perkins wrote in the book, *Welcoming Justice*, that Jesus "spent most of his time discipling twelve men who weren't important in that society. The disciples weren't young scholars preparing for positions in synagogues. They weren't children of the political elite preparing to lead. They were fisherman and tax collectors and failed revolutionaries. They were like so many of the young people in my neighborhood - tossed aside as rejects by society. But Jesus invested his whole ministry in them" (Marsh and Perkins, 76).

The staff who God uses at rescue missions are also just regular people who love the Lord, love people, and merely want to serve. Jesus takes ordinary people to do extraordinary work for His Kingdom. God entrusts the staff at a rescue mission and Christians everywhere to show His love, to share His Gospel, and to bring people into His Church, all of which can be daunting, yet fulfilling tasks. None of this work can be done except by the grace and gifts of a merciful and compassionate God. The work of a rescue mission is indeed difficult work, and on some of the most difficult days, I quoted Philippians 4:13 to myself, "*I can do all things through him who strengthens me.*" We truly can do nothing on our own, but only through the power of God's Holy Spirit.

Author Philip Yancey wrote, "Growing up, Jesus' sensibilities were affected most deeply by the poor, the powerless, the oppressed – in short, the underdogs. Today, theologians debate the aptness of the phrase 'God's preferential option for the poor' as a way of describing God's concern for the underdog. Since God arranged the circumstances in which to be born on planet earth – without power or wealth, without rights, without justice – his preferential options speak for themselves" (Yancey, 41). I also thought about how many of our clients Jesus might someday use to spread His Word and bring others into His Kingdom. After all, God can use anyone to do His work since He is the one who equips people for ministry by giving everyone unique gifts and talents to do the work He desires.

Jesus was born in a smelly barn to a poor teenage woman, and while growing up with his mother Mary and her husband Joseph, the family was still poor. Mary and Joseph made a trip to Jerusalem with the their infant son Jesus as Scripture says: "*When the time came for their purification according to the Law of Moses, they brought him up to Jerusalem to present him to the Lord (as it is written in the Law of the Lord, 'Every male who first opens the womb shall be called holy to the Lord') and to offer a sacrifice according to what is said in the Law of the Lord, 'a pair of turtledoves, or two young pigeons'*" (Luke 2:22-24). What was the "Law of Moses?" According to Leviticus 12, when a woman's "days of purification" are over, she is to, "*Bring the priest at the entrance of the tent of meeting a lamb a year old for a burnt offering, and a pigeon or a turtledove for a sin offering, and he shall offer it before the Lord and make atonement for her. Then she shall be clean from the flow of her blood. This is the law for her who bears a child, either male or female. And if she cannot afford a lamb, then she shall take two turtledoves or two pigeons, one for a burnt offering and the other for a sin offering. And the priest shall make atonement for her, and she shall be clean*" (Leviticus 12:6-8). Since Mary and Joseph did not have a lamb, but instead brought a pair of turtledoves and pigeons, we know they were poor. When Jesus was grown, He never had a home of His own either, but depended on friends to house Him and care for His needs (Matthew 8:20 & Luke 9:57-58).

If we are to be Christ-like, then we too must have a heart for the poor, the homeless, the outcasts, the prostitutes, the drug addicts, the alcoholics, and the lost who unfortunately are most of the men and women who come through the doors of a rescue mission. Mother Teresa once said, "The poor are very great people, they can teach us many beautiful things" ("Inspirational sayings of Mother Teresa" card in Calcutta, India). Perhaps the poor can teach us the heart of God and teach us to love more fully. God gives all of us the strength and the gifts we need to do the work He calls us to do. He wants us all to love Him and others more fully, whether it is at a rescue mission, or any other place He takes us in our lives. Working at a rescue mission though showed me the infinite love of God for very broken and hurting people.

In the gospels, Jesus shows us that He met people where they were, took the time for the unclean and the sinners, offered them forgiveness, but also told them to "*go, and from now on sin no more*" (John 8:11). Jesus loves people far too much to leave them in their sins. He wants to take the people who are often over-looked, ignored, or looked down upon, and give them new life in Him. The work at a mission is to view all people as Jesus does; to love them and help them, but even more, to love the clients enough to point them to a richer and more meaningful life which only comes from knowing Christ and following His Word.

My hope at the mission was to help our clients understand the infinite love of our Savior and His desire for them to become transformed by the power of the Holy Spirit. Through a simple meal, a pair of socks or a coat, hygiene supplies, help finding work, housing, and becoming sober, but mostly giving unconditional love, rescue missions can show desperate people how to put off their old ways of life and live the abundant life Jesus offers to us all which is found in the following words of Peter:

"*Since therefore Christ suffered in the flesh, arm yourselves with the same way of thinking, for whoever has suffered in the flesh has ceased from sin, so as to live for the rest of the time in*

*the flesh no longer for human passions but for the will of God.
For the time that is past suffices for doing what the Gentiles
want to do, living in sensuality, passions, drunkenness, orgies,
drinking parties, and lawless idolatry. With respect to this they
are surprised when you do not join them in the same flood of
debauchery, and they malign you; but they will give account to
him who is ready to judge the living and the dead. For this is why
the gospel was preached even to those who are dead, that though
judged in the flesh the way people are, they might live in the spirit
the way God does. The end of all things is at hand; therefore be
self-controlled and sober-minded for the sake of your prayers.
Above all, keep loving one another earnestly, since love covers
a multitude of sins. Show hospitality to one another without
grumbling. As each has received a gift, use it to serve one another,
as good stewards of God's varied grace: whoever speaks, as one
who speaks oracles of God; whoever serves, as one who serves by
the strength that God supplies – in order that in everything God
may be glorified through Jesus Christ. To him belong glory and
dominion forever and ever. Amen."* (1 Peter 4:1-11).

"We exist to glorify God through a Christ-centered
ministry that meets the physical, emotional and
spiritual needs of hurting people in the
greater Lexington area."

Epilogue

Since 2001, the Lexington Rescue Mission has worked
to rebuild lives that have been broken by poverty. Poverty
steals peace. It crushes dignity. It destroys hope. So in all
that the mission does, they invite people into the presence of
Jesus Christ. He alone offers peace that passes understanding,
the dignity of being a child of God, and lasting hope for
eternity. He is the one who redeems that which is broken. And
through Him, we see lives changed. It often starts with a hot
meal, hygiene supplies, or a warm bed. These simple acts of
compassion can open the door to address the deeper issues that
keep hurting people trapped in poverty and offer real hope for
the future.

The story of how the Lexington Rescue Mission began is
an interesting one from the founders, Jim and Becky Connell.
In late December 1995, Jim Connell was laid-off from his
administrative position at a regional community mental health
organization in south-central Indiana. Jim didn't want to
uproot his family and move away from the community to find
comparable employment, but he thought that would be the
most likely course for him to follow if he wanted to maintain
his standard of living. So, Jim prayed that God would provide
him with a comparable job with a local employer.

Fortunately, the Executive Director who had reluctantly
discharged Jim about a month earlier, called him to say that
he knew of a "perfect" job opportunity that he thought Jim
should consider. The nearby regional hospital helped organize
a Healthy Communities Initiative (HCI), which was led by a
volunteer group of prominent members of the community.
One of the initiatives being led by a subgroup of HCI was
focusing on establishing a clinic to provide free medical care to

low-income, uninsured residents of the community by using volunteer doctors and nurses. This group of volunteers was looking for a project manager to start-up such a clinic.

Jim interviewed for this one-year position and accepted the job since he believed this was God's answer to his prayer. The job would help him develop his project management skills; It would be immensely rewarding personally as he knew he would be helping to launch a long-term service of great value to those who struggled to access the healthcare they needed; and he would be taking on a temporary assignment, which would inevitably stretch his faith in God's continued provision as the job was nearing its end.

Seven months after he started his project management position for "Volunteers in Medicine" (VIM), the clinic opened in a free-standing building near downtown Columbus, Indiana. Opening day was on September 26, 1996. It was a joyous day for Jim. He finished his year with VIM focusing on the operational aspects of the clinic and establishing a medication assistance program for patients with chronic illnesses who could not afford their prescriptions.

About a month before Jim's one-year assignment was due to end, Jim heard that the Director of the regional hospital foundation was resigning from her job. The hospital administrators decided to take the opportunity to enlarge the foundation staff, so they hired a former school administrator to be the next Executive Director and added a new position for their annual fundraising campaigns.

Jim was asked if he would like to apply for that position, and he was hired just as his project management position with VIM ended. No doubt, this might have seemed to be coincidental, or lucky, to many, but Jim knew that God's hand made it all possible. He wasn't sure why God would place a former CPA, Certified Financial Planner, and health care administrator in such a role as this, but he now believes God was equipping him with the skills he should have to be an effective mission director years later.

Jim served from 1997 to 2001 at the hospital foundation. During this time, the Executive Director reached her aggressive endowment campaign goal and decided to retire. As the hospital administration was deciding who would replace her, Jim was asked if he would want to apply for the position. Jim turned down the opportunity because he didn't think this career move would be a good long-term fit for a Christian who wanted to be "all in" for God, while at the same time being effective at cultivating major gifts from many who oppose the truth.

A young lady, who had important social ties along with experience in raising major gifts for an academic institution, was hired as the next foundation director. Soon after she began, it became clear to Jim that she wanted to reshape Jim's job in such a way that would remove much of the job satisfaction that he enjoyed under the former Director's leadership. Jim realized that his value to the foundation was being diminished and that a job change would be inevitable.

In late summer of 2000, Jim looked at what kinds of work seemed most important to him, and he concluded that he had only two areas of high interest—social outreach and evangelism. As he researched the kinds of Christian ministries that interested him, rescue missions stood out to him the most. Rescue Missions have a long history in America. Their goal is to broadly serve those who are less fortunate in our society with the hope of saving many through the gospel.

At that time, there were an estimated 600 or more rescue missions in the country, and nearly half of them were members of the Association of Gospel Rescue Missions (AGRM). So,

Jim contacted the expansion director of AGRM to get some advice for someone, like himself, who thought about starting a mission ministry in a community that needed one. Jim thought his financial and administrative skills could best be utilized in starting a mission rather than joining one. The AGRM staff member responsible for supporting new missions recommended that Jim attend one of the Association's regional conferences as a means to help confirm whether or not he should pursue this.

So one day in the fall of 2000, Becky stopped by Jim's office at the hospital foundation and Jim knew it was time to talk to her about the idea of starting a mission. He knew Becky had a heart to serve the poor and homeless. (Sometime before, when a nonprofit shelter in Seymour was trying to recruit a volunteer director for their program, Becky had considered applying for the position, and she probably would have applied if they hadn't needed the income from the job she already had.)

Jim motioned Becky into his office, shut the door behind them, and told her he thought he knew what God wanted them to do for the rest of their lives. Then, he waited for a response. He knew she would have to agree for this to work out right. Jim and Becky had led the benevolent team at their church. As a registered dietician, Becky organized and led the church's community thanksgiving dinner each year. The idea seemed to be a natural one to Jim, but would Becky be willing to leave everything to follow Jim in such an uncertain path. Jim had previously shared with her several ideas that she couldn't get excited about. How would she respond to one more idea? Her response would undoubtedly determine their ultimate decision.

Her response was unusually receptive to the idea. They both knew that they would need to move from their rather small, affluent community into a city large enough that could support the size of a typical mission, but they didn't want to move so far away that they could not attend to the needs of their aging parents as they might arise. They also knew they should talk to others who had started a mission so they could learn from them.

Since there was a conference coming up soon in Buffalo, New York, Jim decided to go. At the conference, Jim met a wide range of mission employees, including some who started missions. There were harrowing stories shared, but in the end, God's faithfulness always seemed to the ring true. Jim left the conference believing this could be the hardest work he would ever do, but it was surely the work God was calling him to do.

With this conviction in his heart that starting a rescue mission was God's calling on he and his wife, Jim met with two AGRM regional presidents, one who directed the rescue mission in Kokomo, Indiana and the other who directed the mission in Knoxville, Tennessee. His goal was to identify possible communities within those two regions that could benefit from having a rescue mission. From those meetings, he heard about the need for ministries in Ann Arbor, Michigan; Columbus, Ohio; and Lexington, Kentucky.

Jim began reading online newspaper articles about homelessness in each of these three communities. He and Becky were never very excited about moving north to Ann Arbor. (It seemed to be their version of "Nineveh" due to the harsher climate.) In Columbus, Ohio, shelters had become too much of a political "hot potato" since the city was trying to move shelters around so they could better hide the homeless as they pursued economic development.

That left Lexington, Kentucky as a possibility. Jim and Becky both had an affinity toward Kentucky well before this time. Becky grew up on a farm near Corydon, Indiana, which is only 30 miles or so west of Louisville. Her family closely followed Kentucky sports and local news from Louisville. Jim and Becky frequently vacationed at Cumberland Lake. So, Jim planned a trip to Lexington to talk to pastors and nonprofit leaders who could help him understand how a new rescue mission could fit into this community.

Jim was told there were at least 1,000 people homeless in Lexington on any given day, and the large majority of the homeless were males. At the time, there were only two nonprofits that housed most of the homeless population. Homeless women were housed at the Salvation Army and homeless men were housed at the Hope Center. Since homeless men represent the vast majority of people served at rescue missions, Jim took a close look at the need for men's services. He found that the Hope Center in 2000 had a bed capacity of about 115. Yet, they were housing up to about 220 men in beds and on the floor on a cold winter night. It appeared that the demand for services had badly outstripped the supply.

Not only was there a need for more beds and services for homeless men, but there was also no faith ministry providing the existing services. This is not to say that what they were doing wasn't important, because they were certainly providing relief services. But they weren't there to point homeless and addicted men to the saving love of Jesus Christ, who could save their lives for eternity. This was a clear unmet need that was beyond any dispute.

After Jim's trip to Lexington, Jim and Becky prayed over the matter and felt that God was calling them to establish a mission in Lexington. Their son was a Junior in High School at the time, and when asked if he would like to move or stay in Columbus to finish high school, he opted for the latter. Jim and Becky decided that Becky would continue to work and to stay in Columbus with Brian until he was off to college. Jim would move to a 1-bedroom apartment in Lexington and commute to Columbus on most weekends.

Since the Connell's income would be cut nearly in half, Jim asked his supervisor at the hospital foundation if he could ease into this transition by working part-time at the foundation and part-time starting the mission. She replied that it would be better if Jim was either "all in or all out". Although this didn't give Jim the emotional crutch he was looking for, he now knew that any future success in planting a rescue mission would have to come from the hand of God Himself. And, of course, this would bring glory to God.

Jim and Becky were members of Community Church of Columbus (CCC) at the time they were making these decisions. CCC was very supportive of their decision to go, and they remained supportive throughout the whole time Jim and Becky served the Lexington Rescue Mission. On Sunday, April 1, the day Jim moved to Lexington, CCC sent Jim and Becky, with their blessing, as the Connells embarked on this missionary work.

On April 2, 2001, Jim incorporated Lexington Rescue Mission in the Commonwealth of Kentucky. And the rest is history.

Quitting their jobs in Indiana and moving to Kentucky was a leap of faith, but they felt that God was in this move and trusted Him. Jim and Becky wanted to open a rescue mission that was Christ-centered and met three criteria:

1. Meet basic, critical needs of people such as food, clothing, and shelter.
2. Heal people from the inside out, providing intervention in desperate lives, and offer classes and counseling for anyone in need.

3. Give hope for the future which only comes through Jesus Christ.

The mission statement for the Lexington Rescue Mission is, "We exist to glorify God through a Christ-centered ministry that meets the physical, emotional and spiritual needs of hurting people in the greater Lexington area."

The primary goals of the Mission are:

► **CARING FOR THOSE IN NEED:**

People who are hurting will find help meeting their basic needs at the Lexington Rescue Mission. We offer nutritious meals to anyone who is hungry, clothing for those in need, and a place to rest for the weary. All of our guests are invited to meet with our case worker who will help them regain financial stability and take steps out of poverty.

► **PREPARING PEOPLE FOR WORK:**

Men and women who need employment will find help getting back to work at the Lexington Rescue Mission. Our Jobs for Life classes teach the skills necessary to find and keep lasting employment, and graduates are placed in jobs in local businesses so they can provide for themselves and their families.

► **ENDING HOMELESSNESS:**

Helping people get off the streets and out of shelters is at the core of our ministry. We offer transitional housing for homeless men and women who need help getting back on their feet. We also provide housing counseling to help homeless individuals and families move into a home of their own.

► **RESTORING BROKEN LIVES:**

Men and women whose lives have been broken by trauma, addiction, and incarceration can find healing and hope through the Lexington Rescue Mission. We lead classes in jails, prisons, and in the community that get to the root of self-destructive behaviors and offer lasting freedom in Christ.

If Jim and Becky Connell had not followed the prompting of the Lord to leave their comfortable and stable lives in Indiana and move to Lexington, Kentucky to the unknown work of a rescue mission, none of these stories would exist; perhaps none of these lives would have been touched. How important it is to follow the still, small voice of the Lord and allow Him to use us as He desires. Thank you Jim and Becky, and thank you to their daughter Laura, who worked with them through their journey and is now the Executive Director of the mission!

For more information about the Lexington Rescue Mission, please go to their website to learn more about them and how you can donate and volunteer to be a part of this exciting work God has been doing there for more than twenty years!

LexingtonRescue.org

Working at a Rescue Mission
Just Another Day in Paradise

Donna Junker

References

Adams, Marilyn McCord. *Horrendous Evils and the Goodness of God.* Cornell University Press, Ithaca, New York: 1999.

Anderson, Neil T. *Who I Am In Christ.* Bethany House Publishing, Minneapolis, Minnesota: 2001.

Archaeology Study Bible, English Standard Version. Crossway, Wheaton, Illinois: 2017.

Collins, Gary R. *Christian Counseling: A Comprehensive Guide, Third Edition.* Thomas Nelson Publishers, Nashville, Tennessee: 2007

Eiseley, Loren. *The Starfish Thrower.* A Harvest book, Harcourt Publishers, San Diego, California: 1979.

Fikkert, Brian and Russel Mask. *From Dependency to Dignity.* Zondervan, Grand Rapids, Michigan: 2015.

Kasik, Donna. *Recovery: A Return to the Self.* GreenWine Family Books (a division of GlobalEdAdvance Press), Knoxville, Tennessee: 2010.

Manning, Brennan. *The Ragamuffin Gospel: Visual Edition.* Multnomah Publishers, Inc., Sisters, Oregon: 2005.

Marsh, Charles and John Perkins. *Welcoming Justice: God's Movement Toward Beloved Community.* Intervarsity Press, Downers Grove, Illinois: 2009.

Maslow, Abraham. *Psychological Review, "Motivation and Personality"* Harper, New York, New York: 1954.

McGee, Robert S. *The Search for Significance: Seeing Your TRUE WORTH through God's EYES.* Thomas Nelson Publishing, Nashville, Tennessee: 2003.

Merton, Thomas. *The Seven Storey Mountain: An Autobiography of Faith.* A Harvest Book, Harcourt, Inc., Orlando, Austin, New York, San Diego, Toronto, London: 1998.

Mother Teresa Center of the Missionaries of Charity pamphlet, Calcutta, India: 2008.

Mother Teresa. *No Greater Love.* New World Library, Novato, California: 1989.

Nouwen, Henri. *"Adam's Peace" in World Vision Magazine,* August-September 1988.

Nouwen, Henri. *Reaching Out.* Fount/Harper Collins Publishers, London, England: 1996.

Plato. *Great Dialogues of Plato.* Translated by W.H.D. Rouse, Mentor Books, The New American Library of World Literature, Inc. New York, New York: 1956.

Poplin, Mary. *Finding Calcutta: What Mother Teresa Taught Me About Meaningful Work and Service.* InterVarsity Press: Downers Grove, IL. 2008

Ten Boom, Corrie. *Clippings From My Notebook.* BPCC Hazell Books, Aylesbury, Bucks, England: 1982.

Thielicke, Helmut. *A Little Exercise for Young Theologians.* Translated from German by Charles L. Taylor. Eerdmans Publishing Company, Grand Rapids, Michigan: 1962.

Yancey, Philip. *The Jesus I Never Knew.* Zondervan, Grand Rapids Michigan: 1995.

About the Author

Donna Junker currently serves on the Board of Directors at the homeless coalition in Jessamine County, Kentucky. She is an ordained chaplain who worked at the Lexington Rescue Mission as the Pastoral Care Coordinator for about six years and had previously worked as a hospice chaplain for many years. Prior to her work as a chaplain, she owned a construction company and worked in the building trades for over twenty years.

Chaplain Junker has a bachelor's degree in philosophy from North Central College in Naperville, Illinois, and a Master of Divinity from Lombard, Illinois. She worked in two hospitals as a resident chaplain, earning her certification in Clinical Pastoral Education, and is also certified in Thanatology (death, dying and bereavement counseling) and in Christian drug and alcohol counseling.

Chaplain Junker volunteered in Calcutta, India at Mother Teresa's Missionaries of Charity, worked as a hospice chaplain in Zambia, southern Africa, and developed and taught short term intensive classes at seminary for seven years in Kitale, Kenya. She has authored seven other books (see Other Books by Author).

Donna is originally from the Chicago suburbs but currently lives in Nicholasville, Kentucky with her husband, Dr. Paul Junker, along with a dog, a cat, and a turtle. She has one son and daughter in law, and two wonderful grandchildren.

DonnaJunker@roadrunner.com

Working at a Rescue Mission
Just Another Day in Paradise

Donna Junker

Other Books by the Author

Three Weeks in Africa
ISBN: 978-1-935434-13-9

"We as the American hospices are not sent to help the poor African hospices, but to deepen relationships with them, to assess needs and to discover how they function. We can share our knowledge with them, and they in turn can share their knowledge and insight with us." Hospice and Palliative Care is a new concept in Africa, and is established, funded and carried out in different ways than American hospices. The author's 3-pronged purpose in writing this book is to: 1) Approach hospice care from a missional point of view, 2) Share the importance of compassionate, faith-based end-of-life care, and 3) Understand and appreciate Zambia's challenges of hospice and palliative care.

Kenya: A Priority on My Bucket List
ISBN: 978-1-935434-63-4

A list of things to do or accomplish before exiting this life is called a bucket list. One of the items on the author's bucket list was to go somewhere in Africa to see the wild animals in their natural habitat. Little did she know that Kenya, East Africa would become like a second home and would offer far more than a safari ride. Traveling to Kenya seven times, the author gives a detailed account of her experiences and brings to light the clash of cultures which can cause misunderstandings between missionaries and Kenyans. The cross-cultural lessons learned in this book can be applied to missions anywhere.

Recovery: A Return to the Self
ISBN: 978-1-935434-51-1

Using real-life situations, the author demonstrates principles and practices to recover the true self lost along the way. The blueprint the author used in her own recovery is like a roadmap to protect and guide - not just a rule book. As a hospice chaplain, the author witnessed first-hand the wisdom of the dying, but it was after working with the poor and dying in India that she created the spiritual 12-step program outlined in this book.

Thinking Outside the Box ...About Love
ISBN: 978-1-935434-00-5

It begins with seeking and ends with discovery; it is a deeply personal story of warm hopes and cold realities. It is a journey of conviction, compelling both the writer and the reader to look at the world differently and start, Thinking Outside the Box.. About Love. This book tells of Donna in the role of VA Chaplain who demonstrates true, Christian love for the lost and suffering.

First Day Devotions

ISBN 978-1-935434-87-0

In my work as a Chaplain/Pastoral Care Coordinator at the Lexington Rescue Mission in Lexington, Kentucky, part of my job is to write a weekly devotional for the staff. Each Wednesday afternoon I sit in my office, pray, and write my devotion, then email it to all of the staff. Each week several of the Mission staff sends me wonderfully kind and uplifting feedback from my devotions, which I do not deserve, but give glory to God if the devotionals have touched hearts and minds. After doing this part of my job for a couple of months, I decided to compile these devotions into a small book that could be used not only for the staff, but also for clients, and perhaps in homes and churches. I have included many of the devotions written at the Mission in this book and pray God uses them to uplift you.

Meditations: A Collection of Weekly & Holiday Reflections

ISBN 978-1-434535-94-8

As I wrote this book, my prayer was that the reader would not settle for a short devotion each week, with Scripture verses inserted into my thoughts, but that they would take some time every day, to read the words that bring healing, hope and life, which are found in the Word of God – the Holy Bible. If we stake our entire lives and eternity on our Christian faith, we must certainly know what that Faith teaches.

Journey to Recovery: A Return to the Self (Workbook)
ISBN: 978-1-950839-15-5

Recovery is not limited to addictions. Not all people suffer from addictions, but we all suffer from not always living as the people we want to be. Journey to recovery and a return to the self simply involve recovering the person who God created us to be, who many of us have lost along life's journey for many reasons, such as: abandonment, betrayal, pain, addictions, loss, etc. God has a plan for all of our lives and, no matter what the circumstances were surrounding our births, God created each of us as a unique person who He wants in this life. We are all valuable to God, and He wants us to live up to our full potential.

Working at a Rescue Mission
Just Another Day in Paradise

ISBN: 978-1-950839-19-3

The author invites the reader to enter with her into the daily life of working at a mission, discover why Gospel rescue missions are so important, and then meet some of the colorful people she came to know. Chaplain Junker emphasizes that to have physical needs met, the Christian Faith is never forced upon anyone. The stories in this book are the unique experiences she had as Chaplain at the Lexington Rescue Mission (LRM); however, the programs that were implemented, the assistance that was given, and the ideas and philosophies that the LRM utilized can be helpful in any rescue mission, transitional house, or emergency homeless shelter.